Preaching the Heart of God:
The place of pathos in preaching

Mike Mellor

DayOne

Copyright © 2021 by Mike Mellor

First published in Great Britain in 2021 by
DayOne, Ryelands Road, Leominster, HR6 8NZ
Email: sales@dayone.co.uk
Website: www.dayone.co.uk

Scripture taken from the New International Version®. Copyright © 1978 by Hodder & Stoughton. Used by permission. All rights reserved.

The right of Mike Mellor to be identified as the Author of this Work has been asserted by him in accordance with the Copyright, Designs and Patents Act 1988.

All rights reserved. No part of this publication may be reproduced, stored in a retrieval system or transmitted in any form or by any means, electronic, mechanical, photocopying, recording or otherwise, without the prior permission of the publisher or the Copyright Licensing Agency.

British Library Cataloguing in Publication Data
A record for this book is available from the British Library

ISBN: 978-1-84625-694-3

Cover design by Kathryn Chedgzoy

Printed by 4edge

To Paul Pease
Through whom I first heard there was
'good news of great joy'.
For even me.

ENDORSEMENTS

This moving, challenging book should be read by every preacher. My regret is that it was not written earlier. I needed to have read this before I retired from pastoral ministry. It bravely addresses the main weaknesses in evangelical preaching today where correct exegesis and biblical theology have become its dominant and all-important characteristic, sermons have become Bible studies addressing the mind, and so hearts are not burning as they did in Emmaus when the risen Jesus opened the Word and then opened the understanding. It deserves the widest readership.

> **Geoff Thomas was the Pastor of Alfred Place Baptist Church in Aberystwyth, Wales for over 50 years. He is a frequent conference speaker all over the world and holds the position of Visiting Professor of Historical Theology at Puritan Reformed Theological Seminary in Grand Rapids, Michigan.**

Every preacher who reads this book will wish that he had read it sooner. By both biblical argument and a treasury of striking quotations Mike Mellor shows us that real preaching conveys not only the mind of God, but also his heart. He then helps us to see how this can be done both in the pulpit and on the pavement.

> **Stuart Olyott has held pastorates in England, Switzerland and Wales, has preached in conferences on every continent and is the author of a number of books.**

In an age when tone and authenticity are so important, it's madness for any preacher to neglect this short book. I've spent thirty years trying to preach and yet I can honestly say I learnt something on every page.

> **Rico Tice, Senior Minister, All Souls Church, London, and co-author of Christianity Explored**

Mike Mellor has written this excellent book to help us address the problem of dull and lifeless preaching and suggests we need more than mere statements of truth and must speak to the heart. He wants to encourage us to connect meaningfully with people and bring pathos into our preaching.

Stephen Kneale, Pastor at Oldham Bethel Church, blogger and podcaster (www.BuildingJerusalem.blog), author and columnist

This is an excellent book on preaching with feeling. At last, a book that gets to the nub of what is wrong with so much of our modern preaching. Many of us have been taught how to handle the text and to engage with exegetical excellence, and yet so much of what passes for preaching is nothing more than an intellectually stimulating (if we're lucky) theological lecture. A great call to emotional, deeply felt, biblical preaching. Definitely worth a read. Get on it.

Mez McConnell, Senior Pastor of Niddrie Community Church near Edinburgh and Director of *20schemes* which is dedicated to revitalising and planting gospel churches in Scotland's poorest communities

ACKNOWLEDGEMENTS

Plato said that, 'Bees cull their sweets from this flower and this blossom, here and there wherever they can find them. But after, they themselves make the honey which is purely their own.' I have sought to 'cull' from the preaching luminaries over the centuries, and pray the 'honey' produced may prove fresh, as well as sweet and nourishing. But I am most grateful also to gifted preachers still living who are referred to and have contributed to the produce, as well as being indebted to Stephen Kneale, Roger Carswell, Geoff Thomas, JP Earnest and Graham Hind for their encouragement, helpful comments and suggestions.

CONTENTS

	FOREWORD	**9**
INTRODUCTION	CHANNELS	**12**
1	A CORD OF THREE STRANDS	**18**
2	THE PLACE OF EMOTION	**28**
3	THE GOD WHO FEELS	**38**
4	PREACHING THAT CONNECTS	**48**
5	HEART AND MIND	**58**
6	HARD TRUTHS AND MELTING WORDS	**68**
7	PATHOS AND THE SPIRIT	**80**
8	HEAT AND LIGHT	**88**
EPILOGUE	A HEART AFTER GOD'S OWN	**100**
APPENDIX 1	PATHOS ON THE STREETS	**107**
APPENDIX 2	TEN ESSENTIAL BOOKS FOR YOUNG PREACHERS	**119**
	ENDNOTES	**123**

FOREWORD

As I write this, we are in the midst of a global pandemic. I am reminded that conservative evangelicals are facing their own long-standing epidemic—boring preaching! Many of us have grown used to dull and lifeless preaching, insisting it is excellent because it is ultimately sound. One reason for this problem is a failure to adequately apply biblical truth to the lives of those listening; we teach the facts of Scripture without making clear how they affect the people listening. Underlying that problem is a failure to connect with those listening. We are quick to explain but not apply, biblical truth gets baldly stated without much sense that we feel it nor that those listening should do either. In short, we lack pathos.

Mike Mellor has written this excellent book to help us address the problem. He wants to encourage us to connect meaningfully with people and bring pathos into our preaching. He suggests we need more than mere statements of truth and must speak to the heart. In this helpful book, Mike encourages us to have a real love for the people to whom we speak and to take care, not just in what we say, but how we say it. People may not always remember what we say, but they will often remember how we said it. If we lack passion for Christ, it will show. If we don't care for the people to whom we preach, it will show. Mike does an excellent job in helping us take some necessary steps away from the boring preaching that still exists in too many places toward that which meaningfully connects and engages the heart. The UK is a country for whom the word 'pathetic' remains an insult, but if we take seriously Mike's call for greater pathos in our preaching, we may just find the Lord mightily uses our pathetic efforts for his glory.

Stephen Kneale, Pastor at Oldham Bethel Church, blogger and podcaster (www.BuildingJerusalem.blog), author and columnist.

Foreword →

Channels

IN THIS CHAPTER

The preacher and the world around him →

The importance of emotional involvement →

The two elements of Pathos →

Introduction

> Therefore we are ambassadors for Christ, as though God were making His appeal through us.
>
> –2 Cor. 5:20

> A Jesus who never wept could never wipe away my tears.[1]
>
> –C.H. Spurgeon

True preaching is not a natural activity. Yes, it involves a man who, having laboured in preparation, is now about to 'stand and deliver'. But it is something much greater and more glorious. True preaching is 'God making his appeal through us' (2 Cor. 5:20). Just dwell on that preacher. God in you, imploring, beseeching pleading with flawed, wayward men and women through your equally flawed and wayward humanity. Not that we are only about entreating our hearers evangelistically of course. As we seek to preach and teach the 'whole counsel of God' from Scripture, 'Some passages', as Haddon Robinson says, 'are alive with hope. Some warn, some create a sense of joy, some flash with anger at injustice, others surge with triumph.'[2]

Our senses these days are blitzed by news flying at us 24/7 in high definition from all over the globe. We stand in constant need of having to guard against emotional overload on the one hand, or becoming callous and desensitized on the other. But, it is good to ask ourselves, 'How does God feel about this?' The terrorist bombing which has just swept dozens of young people out of this world? The guilt-laden mass of 'worshippers' thronging their way to a polluted Indian river in an attempt to wash away their sin? The sacrificial labours of bomb-blitzed medical staff in an ill-equipped hospital? The desperately poor Christian brick kiln workers in Pakistan, languishing on death row over some trumped-up charge? Surely, whatever enters through our eyes and ears must have some effect upon our emotions, otherwise we are no better than robots. But it takes a certain courage to make ourselves vulnerable enough to feel something of the pain. To feel something of the anguish our Saviour so clearly experienced as he moved about the broken wreckage of humanity throughout his days on earth.

Emotional involvement

As preachers we are called to regularly stand and minister to frazzled, fearful, precious beings. (Doubly challenging if having to do this through a camera lens.) Each one listening to our words is struggling with some burden of care and it is our responsibility to bring the Word of God to them. How can we—how *dare* we bring divine truths without being moved by them in any way. Mostyn Roberts highlights not only the challenge, but the glorious high calling that is ours, 'Where does the message come from? We may say, I hope without irreverence, from the heart of God ... Preaching is a matter of three hearts: from the heart of God, through the heart of the preacher, to the heart of the listener.'[3]

If that is so, we must ask ourselves if we are being faithful ambassadors by simply imparting truth when there is little heart-engagement with our hearers? What more pitiful sound on earth can there be than a preacher whose emotions appear to have been so cauterized that there is no appropriate flow of love, grief, anger or compassion from his heart and lips?

Ian Pitt-Watson former professor at Fuller Theological Seminary argues:

> Unless there is some measure of emotional involvement on the part of the preacher and on the part of his hearers, the kerygma [proclamation/preaching] cannot be heard in its fullness for the kerygma speaks to the whole man, emotions and all, and simply does not make sense to the intellect and the will alone.[4]

It can be all too easy to allow our senses to be dulled and fall into a repetitious 'preparation and preaching' rut. To simply deliver 'a word' without having our whole being engaged. This however, has been the challenge facing God's servants throughout the centuries. Pastor and theologian James W. Alexander, concerned about the lack of emotional involvement in the preaching of his day (that is, the nineteenth century) lamented, 'Our young men do not gird themselves for it with the spirit of those who are on the eve of a great conflict; nor do they prepare as those who lay their hands upon the springs of the mightiest passions, and stir up to the depths the ocean of human feelings.'[5]

But it is undoubtedly a twenty-first century problem

also. Mez McConnell, Director of 20schemes (a mission dedicated to revitalising and planting gospel churches in Scotland's poorest communities) pleads, 'Gentlemen, in preaching we do like precision but when we get to Jesus let's see—and hear—more passion.'[6]

This is a challenge preachers face regardless of generation, social class or educational background. Thankfully, it is no problem for God. Two men who are being greatly used today are Rico Tice and Mez McConnell (quoted above). Mez experienced the pain of abuse and rejection in early life. Rico, the privilege of coming from a good family and enjoying the benefits of a public-school education. Two men from two very different worlds. Both could have become victims of their 'systems' but were transformed by the power of Jesus Christ. Both now are passionate preachers of his gospel, overflowing with the grace of God and reaching an audience the breadth of which they perhaps could never have dreamed. To handle God's word faithfully and effectively means (in Pitt-Watson's words) preaching in a manner that 'speaks to the whole man, emotions and all'. It is for this reason that we will be exploring what *pathos* is and why it is so important. And by God's grace, all we who preach will speak words that come, as Mostyn Roberts suggests, 'from the heart of God, through the heart of the preacher, to the heart of the listener'.

Two elements

In our focus on the *pathos* needed for this hour, we will identify two elements—the human and the divine. As men, we are to strive to be those who communicate with the human emotion and passion appropriate to the particular truth we are preaching and situation to which we have been called. But then there is that all important 'extra' we earnestly pray will rest upon our ministries, the Holy Spirit clothing our frail words with something of heaven's dew. The good news is that all of heaven is on our side when we earnestly seek to be channels through which the Holy Spirit can flow. The God of all grace needs no persuading to bless. It is our comfort that God's word 'will not return empty' and that in spite of our often woefully deficient efforts, it 'will accomplish what he desires' (Isa. 55:11). But it is *pathos,* both human and divine, that our world stands in desperate need of right now. However, so often it comes at a price to the preacher, and only spreads its precious fragrance when, like certain flowers, he is crushed. Perhaps we come to this subject weighed down with a sense of guilt, deadness, dryness or failure. But our confidence always rests in the God who forgives, makes alive, refreshes and delights in using those who humbly come with their weakness so all may clearly see that 'this all-surpassing power is from God and not from us' (2 Cor. 4:7). Could it be that the trials or heartache you have experienced are all part of God's preparation to equip you to be his mouthpiece to this broken generation? A broken world needs broken preachers. Rather than feeling weighed down by a sense of unworthiness, we come with all our brokenness and persistent inner struggles, seeing these as things that qualify rather than disqualify us for the work.

A cord of three strands

IN THIS CHAPTER
The preacher and his integrity →
The preacher and his message →
The preacher and his delivery →

Chapter 1 ➡

A cord of three strands is not quickly broken.
>   –Eccles. 4:12

Truth engages the citadel of the human heart and is not satisfied until it has conquered everything there.[1]
>   – A.W. Tozer

Ethos, logos, pathos

The Greek philosopher Aristotle provided a helpful breakdown of effective speech. He divided rhetoric (persuasive public speaking) into three parts: ethos, logos and pathos. Ethos emphasises the integrity or credibility of the speaker; logos concerns the content of the message (for us, Scripture); and pathos concerns the emotions of the speaker. It is pathos which is the focus of this book, the 'how' of the message which we seek to communicate. We may be satisfied that we are faithful in our preaching and teaching and yet are neglectful in this vital area. Despite the privilege that may be ours of having been nurtured in a Scripture-honouring church, we preachers may also be victims of our particular church culture. Some of us can be doctrinally sound, but dry as dust in our delivery. Or, we may be zealous 'thunderers', or quintessentially polite Brits with our calm, clipped delivery. Other factors such as temperament and education will also inevitably play their part. But these must be helps not hindrances to us. We have a timeless message of hope to bring to an increasingly fragile and vulnerable world. Yet in an age of spiritual ignorance, we dare not be guilty of compromise by tinkering with the logos of God. However, the tone we use in communicating it is perhaps the greatest challenge not only for preachers, but for all Christians who seek to make God known. So, let us start by considering the three-fold cord of ethos, logos and pathos, in particular, how they relate to one another, and how we should view them as inseparable friends.

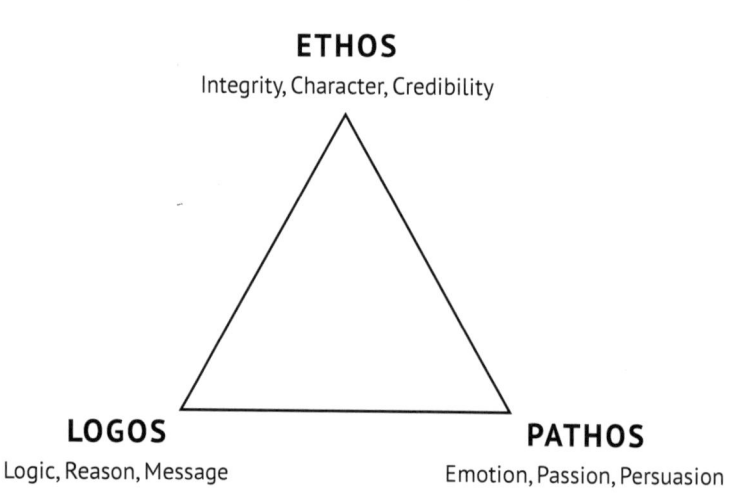

ETHOS
Integrity, Character, Credibility

LOGOS
Logic, Reason, Message

PATHOS
Emotion, Passion, Persuasion

Ethos

We are talking here about the preacher's integrity, his personal life. Charles Spurgeon, urging his seminary students to keep a careful watch over their lives when in the ministry, tells the story of the man who 'preached so well and lived so badly, that when he was in the pulpit everybody thought he ought never to come out again, and when he was out of it, they all declared he never ought to enter it again'.² A humorous story, but warning of a deadly peril. In recent years we have witnessed the tragic downfall of a number of Christian leaders—some eminent men with highly effective ministries. This shrieks to us a solemn fact we must never forget. No matter how many years we might have been engaged in preaching, counselling or other forms of Christian service, we never advance beyond that daily battle with sin that all believers must engage in. The demise of a leader is rarely sudden, there has normally been an inward decay steadily advancing over a period of time. But even if we escape the shame of a sudden public ministerial collapse, we may allow a subtle spiritual bleed over a course of time which will have a similar outcome. The fact is, if we lack integrity, we undermine credibility. If ethos is neglected, logos and pathos are affected. Referring to the Apostle Paul's appeal to 'watch your life and doctrine closely' (1 Tim. 4:16), puritan pastor Richard Baxter warned that, 'One proud, offhand word, one needless contention, one covetous action may cut the throat of many a sermon and blast the fruit of all you have been doing.'

Ethos then refers to the person—our character, what we really are when alone and no one is watching. However, ethos is more than moral integrity. It encompasses also the gifting and competence of the preacher. Integrity is compromised also where there is a lack of gifting which is part of God's calling and equipping of the man. When applying Aristotle's principle to the highest level of speech, for instance, a herald of the gospel, then we must consider his suitability for the task and his diligence in it. The preacher must be both suitably gifted for, and fully committed to, the work. Then it is vital that others recognise, endorse and authorise his aptness. Paul again, writing to Timothy urges, 'Do your best to present yourself to God as one approved, a worker who does not need to be ashamed and who correctly handles the word of truth' (2 Tim. 2:15). We who preach 'will either be approved or ashamed', cautions Warren Wiersbe.[3] A man engaged in this work may perhaps lack the education and eloquence this world makes much of, but a sense of being sent by God and knowing heaven's blessing upon his life and labours can make up for any shortfall. However, one thing that cannot be lacking is ethos—credibility. It is plain to see then, why this particular strand of the three-fold cord is so important. Especially when applied to the life of one whose responsibility it is to exegete and then communicate the Word of God. No wonder we cry with the Apostle, 'Who is equal to such a task?' (2 Cor. 2:16). Thankfully, Paul does not stop there but goes on to point to the work of the Holy Spirit who empowers and equips those who by nature are so deficient in and of themselves—as we shall see later.

Logos

The second part of Aristotle's three-piece rhetoric jigsaw is logos. Whereas ethos refers to the speaker's personal character, logos stresses the importance of appeal to logic. That is, seeking to persuade the hearer by means of reason. The philosopher used the term to refer to a 'reasoned discourse' or 'the argument'. However, we lift the thought once more to its highest expression by seeing logos as the Word of God, Scripture, and then pointing to Christ the living and eternal Logos. Paul is seen demonstrating this in the synagogue in Thessalonica as, 'he *reasoned* with them from the Scriptures, *explaining* and *proving* that the Messiah had to suffer and rise from the dead' (Acts 17:2-3). And then in Athens, 'he was greatly distressed to see that the city was full of idols. So, he *reasoned* in the synagogue with both Jews and God-fearing Greeks, as well as in the marketplace day by day with those who happened to be there' (Acts: 17:16-17). But Paul was not in the slightest interested in bringing his own ideas, as was the practice of the pagans in Athens. In stark contrast, he constantly declared God's logos to all. Without the 'bedrock' of Scripture to stand on, we have no message or authority. Martin Luther testified, 'From the beginning of my Reformation I have asked God to send me neither dreams, nor visions, nor angels, but to give me the right understanding of His Word, the Holy Scriptures; for as long as I have God's word, I know that I am walking in His way and that I shall not fall into any error or delusion.' So, emphasis upon imparting truth and allowing the hearer's mind to digest and examine it is vital. But it is not enough. 'It is *feeling* which gives to words and thoughts their power', stressed John Angell James.[4]

Pathos

'Thank you for waiting. Your call is important to us.' Somehow, we are not too convinced when hearing that message repeated for the ninth time. Our world is becoming increasingly depersonalised and there are occasions when we simply long to speak to a human being rather than being 'put through the system'. It is pathos that conveys the importance, reality and conviction of the message. It is the truth personalised, clothed in flesh and blood. Truth that lives and breathes! Most are familiar with the now famous definition of preaching given long ago by Phillips Brooks, 'Truth brought through personality.' By 'personality' Brooks had in mind character, as opposed to charisma. Charisma is the image which usually registers in our minds when the word is used in today's personality-driven world. God has chosen to communicate through words, written and spoken and has ordained that mere mortals should convey his vital revelation to mankind. Amazingly, those spoken words come to people through a human voice. Like a thumbprint or DNA code, our voice is a unique gift. Whether you like the sound of it or not, your voice is exclusively yours and it sets you apart from any other person. It has been said that the preacher's job is to 'comfort the disturbed and disturb the comfortable'. There are times when that voice must bring healing, and at other times awakening. We can only imagine how Christ sounded when he commanded Lazarus to 'Come forth!' from the tomb. Or in that tension-filled room when, to a dead child, the Lord of life spoke those words, 'Talitha koum' (Little girl, arise). And in what tone did he speak those great words of invitation, 'Come to me all you who are weary and burdened, and I will give you rest' (Matt. 11:28)? We are living in a postmodern culture which (rightly or wrongly) places much emphasis upon emotions. It's not just what we say, it is *how* we say it.

Friends and tripods

Ethos, logos and pathos then are inseparable friends that need each other, and ought never to have a wedge driven between them. Or, to change the imagery. Just as a photographer needs three legs of equal length for his tripod to prevent it being unstable—or worse, collapsing entirely—so the preacher must have the three legs of ethos, logos and pathos firmly in place. Whilst being careful not to undermine the necessity of ethos and pathos, it seems to me the great weakness in preaching in our day is the neglect of pathos. In other words, we can be truth-strong but emotion-weak. When we look back at those heroes we so admire and love to quote—Whitefield, Wesley, Moody, M'Cheyne, Simeon, Lloyd-Jones, Stott and the like—we note a warmth, conviction, intensity, persuasion, indeed, a pathos in their preaching which gave the spoken word such powerful entry into the lives of their hearers. There seems to be a thread connecting these men, regardless of time, denomination, education or temperament. Their preaching was marked by pathos both human and divine. Yet, although they were men who spoke feelingly, they were not content to simply preach truth. They looked to God for more. That something 'extra' accompanying their words, something only God can supply. But whether preaching or seeking to informally bring God's word to a neighbour, friend or work colleague we should pray that the truth coming from our lips might be heart-melting, sorrow-healing, sin-delivering, hope-inducing, lethargy-awakening and above all, God-honouring. To this end, the remaining chapters will be a focus on the all-vital pathos that our world is in desperate need of. We will see how we might be equipped to bring something of the compassionate heart of Christ to a generation that is desperately lost and broken, and yet is totally ignorant to exactly why it is lost and broken, and what the solution might be.

A cord of three strands

The place of emotion

IN THIS CHAPTER
Avoiding boring preaching →
Avoiding manipulative preaching →
Avoiding emotionless preaching →

Chapter 2 ➡

For, as I have often told you before and now say again even with tears.
—Phil. 3:18

I sometimes find myself wishing that (today's) preachers could learn to weep again, but either our tear springs have dried up or our tear ducts have become blocked.[1]
—John Stott

In seeking to emphasise the importance of pathos we are presuming that the one preaching has a high view of Scripture, that it is God's inerrant and infallible word. It is a cause for much thankfulness at this time that men are being raised up and trained who are convinced of the primacy of preaching and teaching. They have the old apostolic conviction that their priority in ministry is to give themselves to 'prayer and the ministry of the word' (Acts 6:4). The church has always been most powerful and had greatest impact when this is the case. Yet the pendulum is always swinging and whilst in these days there is a renewed emphasis on logos, there appears, as we have said, a neglect regarding pathos. We can be careful exegetes of the word and yet negligent in those vital elements of emotion, passion and persuasion in our preaching and teaching ministries.

Dull and boring?

In appealing for 'speaking that glows', former Rector of All

Souls, Langham Place in London, Richard Bewes, quotes the 'sit up and listen' preaching of Australian John Chapman who said, 'Every occasion has got to be like an ace down the centre line.' Bewes continues, 'There will be a glow and a captivation about our messages when the speaker and the audience can share together in their awareness that they are caught up in something that is infinitely bigger than themselves.'[2] The searching question is: Why is there such a lack of preaching that 'glows' today? Another Anglican Jonathan Mason comments, 'Many preachers—at least in Britain—use limited emotional appeal. This may have something to do with English "reserve": we don't express our emotions in public. It may also have something to do with the university education that many of us have been through and the public school upbringing of many of our best-known models.'[3] But this is certainly not a denominational problem. Dr Martyn Lloyd-Jones would complain in his day about Reformed non-conformist preachers who were 'dull and boring'. And there is little evidence that things have changed for the better. 'There is something radically wrong with dull and boring preachers,' he complained. 'How can a man be dull when he is handling such themes? I would say that a "dull preacher" is a contradiction in terms; if he is dull he is not a preacher. He may stand in a pulpit and talk, but he is certainly not a preacher.'[4] John Bunyan witnessed tears streaming down the cheeks of his listeners. He then reveals the reason for this, 'I preached what I felt, what I smartingly did feel, even that under which my poor soul did groan and tremble to astonishment.' Bunyan didn't convey truth in any detached or dispassionate manner, but he himself was deeply affected by the truth he handled, his whole being was involved. However, there was an inevitable and unavoidable personal cost and it was not comfortable. He tells us he 'smartingly' felt it, but surely this is the incomparable thrill of being God's channel, embodying the truth we ourselves believe, feel and want to sincerely convey. Can we expect our hearers to be gripped by our subject if we ourselves are not? If the truth has not moved us, it will not move them. Then there is the danger that if we are men who hold theological convictions (and we will be) we can be so anxious to avoid error in our delivery that our speech is stiff and stilted—even, bland and boring. In other words, the fire is so guarded that it gives off no heat.

Manipulation

We are rightly wary of manipulators. We have seen them powerfully at work in the worlds of marketing, politics and entertainment. But it is particularly repulsive when we see manipulation doing its devious work in the religious sphere. It is nothing new of course. Paul was anxious to distance himself from the spiritual wheeler-dealers of his day, asserting, '... we have renounced secret and shameful ways; we do not use deception, nor do we distort the word of God. On the contrary, by setting forth the truth plainly we commend ourselves to everyone's conscience in the sight of God' (2 Cor. 4:2). We are conscious also of others in the church today who may be sincere but mistake perspiration for inspiration, thinking that a raised voice and flailing arms will add impact to their words. The 'weak point, speak louder' approach. Not that any of this should cause us to overact and jettison rhetoric, which like print or the Internet can be used for good or evil. One helpful definition of rhetoric is, 'The art or study of using language effectively and persuasively.'[5] Surely the aim of every preacher is to be effective and persuasive, and to have an impact upon our hearers. We should shun that laziness which gives no effort to the way we present the truth we so highly esteem, and labour at using language which will most effectively convey it. Arguing for use of true eloquence, Blaise Pascal says, 'Eloquence is the art of saying things in such a way that those to whom we speak may listen to without pain and with pleasure.'[6] We certainly see plenty of God-inspired rhetoric in the Old Testament prophets, and indeed in the preaching and teaching of the Lord Jesus Christ. We see him employing powerful images to make the truth plain. He speaks of salt, light, planks, birds, flowers, vines, branches, fruit for example. Seeking to ensure even the simplest in the audience could understand, the master teacher engaged his hearers by using picture language. The Apostle to the Gentiles likewise would speak about slaves, soldiers, marriage and athletics to drive home the truth. There is truth in the old Arabic proverb, 'He is the best speaker who can turn men's ears into eyes.' It is helpful to keep in mind that 'the mind of man is a picture gallery, not a debating chamber.'[7] So, we should labour to give our hearers vision whilst imparting information.

Personality power

Another fear we may wrestle with is the reliance on 'personality power'. We see churches that appear biblical and yet seem to be built upon the sheer dynamism and charisma of an individual. Of course, there is inevitably a tension here, as in Scripture we clearly see the wide variety of characters and personalities used by God. In fact, it is the diversity and absence of cultish clone-like methodology that adds to the credibility of our message. However, it is painful as well as perilous when a preacher upstages the one he professes to represent. But who is entirely guiltless here? We all, sadly have to confess there are times in our preaching when we are overtaken by our earthly natures and have found ourselves thinking we are capable of doing the job quite well without the Spirit's aid, thank you very much!

Martyn Lloyd-Jones warns:

> A man prepares a message and, having prepared it, he may be pleased and satisfied with the arrangement and order of the thoughts and certain forms of expression. If he is of an energetic, fervent nature, he may well be excited and moved by that and especially when he preaches the sermon. But it may be entirely of the flesh and have nothing at all to do with spiritual matters. Every preacher knows

exactly what this means ... You can be carried away by your own eloquence and by the very thing you yourself are doing and not by the truth at all.

There seems to be something quite paradoxical in Lloyd-Jones' view of preaching here. On the one hand he is saying that one's personality is important in the delivery ('truth through personality') and then on the other he says that the man should 'disappear'. The point he is making is that the preacher is a channel for the Holy Spirit and there should be no rivalry. As Scottish theologian James Denney famously put it: 'In preaching you cannot produce at the same time the impression that you are clever and that Christ is wonderful.'

Use of God-given emotions

But the man and the way he delivers the message really does matter. By 'pathos' I am arguing, on the human level, for a legitimate, appropriate display of passion from the preacher. It is a fallen, fallible being delivering God's truth through God-given emotions consistent with that person's character and temperament. It is not difficult to see where this is *not* happening. Cold preaching produces cold Christians. Heartless preaching produces heartless Christians. Lethargic preaching produces lethargic Christians. But passionate preaching will produce passionate Christians. Church history provides us with a rich and at times surprising array of personalities and temperaments God has greatly used who have expressed

The place of emotion

pathos in keeping with (at times despite) their natural selves. No one argued more strongly, and was so heavily criticised for the use of emotion than Jonathan Edwards—perhaps the greatest philosopher and theologian the United States has produced—yet many today might well be critical of his sermon delivery style. He is recorded as preaching with a candle in one hand and eyes firmly fixed on his sermon notes which he held in the other. Nonetheless the passion and pathos expressed in his preaching could at times be overwhelming. A man who had heard Edwards preach was asked if he was an eloquent preacher. The reply was:

> He had no studied varieties of the voice, and no strong emphasis. He scarcely gestured, or even moved; and he made no attempt by the elegance of his style, or the beauty of his pictures, to gratify the taste, and fascinate the imagination. But, if you mean by eloquence, the power of presenting an important truth before an audience, with overwhelming weight of argument, and with such intenseness of feeling, that the whole soul of the speaker is thrown into every part of the conception and delivery; so that the solemn attention of the whole audience is riveted, from the beginning to the close, and impressions are left that cannot be effaced; Mr. Edwards was the most eloquent man I ever heard speak.[8]

➡ Preaching the Heart of God

Chalk and cheese

To continue to illustrate that pathos is not dependent upon temperament or personality, consider briefly George Whitefield and John Wesley. Whitefield was a warm-hearted 'people-person', whereas Wesley was known to have a difficult personality, he even had the capacity (as one has said) to 'fall out with his own shadow'. However, both men were passionate, fervent men filled with the Spirit and incredibly used by God in the eighteenth-century evangelical awakening that shook the nation. Whitefield was often accused of being an actor with his electrifying preaching, and while his style was different, Wesley also preached to multitudes who gathered to hang on his every word. The point is, both preached with a pathos that could disarm even their fiercest opponents. And there were many. Both were often pelted with stones, dirt, and worse! Wesley was a neat, fastidious man, dressed in clerical robes throughout his ministry—and no doubt did not delight in such opposition to him and his message, standing to preach before his audience covered in mud and blood. But the love of Christ within him could produce a remarkable change in his adversaries. One day, pursued by yet another angry mob, they rushed toward him as he stood on a chair to preach, and as he records in his journal, 'My heart was filled with love, my eyes with tears, and my mouth with arguments.' He then describes how a solemn hush came over the crowd, 'They were amazed; they were ashamed; they were melted down; they devoured every word.'[9] Of course, pathos will look different depending on the context and particular area of ministry. For example, observing a pastor preach to his people in the Philippines (reckoned among the world's most emotional people) will look very different to a Russian pastor preaching to his people (reckoned among the least emotional). And then congregations and temperament within any one country will vary also. The area in which we minister and the class and education of those to whom we preach must inevitably be thrown into the mix. But as stated earlier, we are appealing for an '*appropriate* display of passion from the preacher'. So, what might be fitting for my church may well seem odd or even inappropriate for yours. The point is, as preachers we should earnestly endeavour to convey not just the mind of God as revealed in his word, but his heart also. That is, how he *feels*. But are we justified in the use of such language?

The God who feels

IN THIS CHAPTER

The Passibility of God →
The God who feels →
The God of all comfort →

Chapter 3

Praise be to the God and Father of our Lord Jesus Christ, the Father of compassion and the God of all comfort ...

–2 Cor. 1:3

The Lord accommodates himself to the manner of men, by attributing to himself all the affection, love, and compassion which a father can have.

–John Calvin

It is important for us to do a little drilling down theologically in this chapter to see if there might be any possible doctrinal reason for a lack of pathos-flow in a preaching ministry. Preaching can often be defective or weak because of bad doctrine. Other times good doctrine might be in place but application is skewed.

The doctrine of the passibility of God has to do with the theology of the 'suffering' of God and addresses the question, 'Does God suffer?' That is, can he truly feel emotional pain? Christian orthodoxy has taught that God is *im*passible—that is, He is not subject to suffering, pain or impulsive passions. The Westminster Confession of Faith states that God is 'without body, parts, or passions, immutable'. We make an enormous mistake if we project our humanity onto God (to say, 'I feel like this, therefore God must too.') We cannot base our theology upon human experience and project our image onto God. But we fall into equal error if we conclude that God is detached and unconcerned. Anglican theologian J. I. Packer argues, 'A totally impassive God would be a horror, and not the God of Calvary at all. He might belong in Islam; he has no place in Christianity. If, therefore, we can learn to think of the chosenness of God's grief and pain as the essence of his impassibility, so-called, we will do well.'[1] It is not hard to see why the doctrine of divine impassibility has been so defended by Scripture-honouring saints through the centuries. We want to see God as totally detached from the mayhem of this fallen word, unruffled, unaffected, unassailable. Which of course he is. The early church fathers linked God's impassibility to the doctrine of his immutability, that is God cannot change or be changed. But they did not mean in their teaching that God is devoid of emotion. The point Packer forcibly makes is that a God who is unmoved by suffering could not be the God of Scripture. The God of the incarnation and the cross, and that impassibility simply means that 'God's experiences do not come upon him as ours come upon us.'[2] Dane Ortland, who seeks to take us 'to the heart of Christ' in his book *Gentle and Lowly* writes, 'Let us not dishonour God by so emphasising his transcendence that we lose a sense of the emotional life of God of which our own emotions are an echo, even if a fallen and distorted echo.'[3]

The prophets

In the Old Testament, we see men called and sent to speak on behalf God. They come weeping (Jeremiah) and pleading with his people in all their adulterous filth to return to him.

The God who feels

Often with astonishing tenderness (Hosea). Why did the Holy One of Israel instruct his servants not only to preach but, at times, to actually act out the message before the people? Even to the extent of commanding Hosea to take an unfaithful harlot wife, and then endure the ongoing shame! Was it not for the reason that they might grasp how he 'feels'? I had the privilege of studying Old Testament under the respected Hebrew scholar John Waite. I plainly remember the day, seated in that small lecture hall in South Wales Bible College, eagerly anticipating another of his vibrant lectures. We had just started working through Isaiah, when I was hit by his comments on the fourth verse of the first chapter which opens with the prophet's stark and devastating analysis regarding the state of the nation. Putrid from head to toe:

> Ah, sinful nation,
>   a people laden with iniquity,
> offspring of evildoers,
>   children who deal corruptly!
> They have forsaken the Lord,
>   they have despised the Holy One of Israel,
>   they are utterly estranged. (Isa. 1:4)

My understanding of God here—fist-shaking and teeth-clenched—was shattered as the college Principal explained that in his anger and revulsion at their rebellion, the 'Ah' (Heb. *hoy*) expressed and comprised a sense of grief. It is a deep groan conveying compassion, sorrow and broken-heartedness as well as anger as he sees his people in their waywardness. Is it unreasonable to view this response so far removed from that of the Father of the prodigal the Lord Jesus so graphically portrays, as the young son he loves snatches, flees and then blows his inheritance with such brazen and debauched depravity? This is the God who rebukes the sulky prophet Jonah who was more concerned about a plant than those to whom God had sent him! 'But the LORD said, "You have been concerned about this vine, though you did not tend it or make it grow. It sprang up overnight and died overnight. But Nineveh has more than a hundred-and-twenty-thousand people who cannot tell their right hand from their left, and many cattle as well. Should I not be concerned about that great city?"' (Jonah 4: 10–11). This is the God who unashamedly derives pleasure from his creation. Before the fall we are told he 'saw all that he had made, and it was very good' (Gen. 1:31). And of course, it is no surprise that he found delight in his Son, 'And a voice from heaven said, "This is my Son, whom I love; with him I am well pleased"' (Matt. 3:17). But perhaps most difficult to accept is how he could possibly find pleasure in those who caused that beloved Son to die. How utterly startling is that picture of the singing God delighting in those who are far from delightful. 'The LORD your God is in your midst, a mighty one who will save; he will rejoice over you with gladness; he will quiet you by his love; he will exult over you with loud singing' (Zeph. 3:17 ESV).

God indifferent to pain and suffering?

Theologian Donald MacLeod comments, 'If God derives pleasure from His creation, He is also moved by its plight, and particularly the plight of His people.' Macleod then proceeds to refer to the distress of God's people in bondage in Egypt, 'The Lord said, "I have indeed seen the misery of my people in Egypt. I have heard them crying out because of their slave drivers, and I am concerned about their suffering."' (Exod. 3:7)

McLeod then quotes Bible commentator Alec Motyer who writes of, '... the sensitive feeling which makes the Lord aware of Israel's plight, and the graciousness which prompts Him to identify with them in their need'.[4]

Surely the prophet Isaiah takes us to the very heart of God when he says:

> In all their affliction he was afflicted,
>> and the angel of his presence saved them;
>> in his love and in his pity he redeemed them;
>> he lifted them up and carried
>>> them all the days of old. (Isa. 63:9 ESV)

John Calvin, referring to this passage says that God, 'was so careful about them that he himself bore their distresses and afflictions. By speaking in this manner, he declares the incomparable love which God bears toward his people. In order to move us more powerfully and draw us to himself, the Lord accommodates himself to the manner of men, by attributing to himself all the affection, love, and compassion which a father can have.'[5] Though Calvin was in the divine impassibility camp, he says that it is out of sheer love and gracious condescension that God reveals himself to us in human terms. Theologians, when speaking on God's 'emotional' life often use the term 'anthropopathism'. (This is in contrast to 'anthropomorphism' where the Bible uses human terms speaking of God physically, having hands, feet, nostrils, breath, etc.) So, while there is nothing that takes him by surprise or could possibly overwhelm him, yet he is not unmoved by the suffering of those he has created, and in particular, the distress of his covenant people.

The God of all comfort

The Apostle Paul seeks to encourage the believers in Corinth by reminding them that the God who saved them and to whom they belong is, 'the Father of compassion and the God of all comfort' (2 Cor. 1:3). Paul testifies to God's grace given to him personally in distressing times—and for a greater purpose—that others may benefit in the flow of compassion. It comes from God, 'who comforts us in all our troubles, so that we can comfort those in any trouble with the comfort we ourselves receive from God.' We are able to cheer and hearten others in their trials, not because we are inherently compassionate people (far from it, we can be hard-hearted and self-centred), but rather, we are channels through which comfort can flow from a bottomless source, the Father of compassion. Every conversion is a miracle of divine grace. It is God coming to one whose entire focus has been upon sin and self and completely revolutionising that life in such a way that he or she desires to think and act as God himself does. Because my own conversion was sudden and dramatic, the change in priorities was all the more sudden and noticeable. Going to work in the morning, a hopeless, dying alcoholic, then trusting Christ and immediately returning home rejoicing, bursting with hope, having been given new aims and ambitions. I drove home that day bathed in tears of joy, overwhelmed by the love of God, knowing he had forgiven me; knowing Christ had died for me; knowing that if I had a fatal car crash that day, I would go to heaven. But I was still on earth and was about to face a mystified wife!

Changed priorities

Opening the door—my wife was in the kitchen—I called to her, 'Gwen, I've become a Christian!' Her head sunk into her hands and she gasped to herself, 'Oh, no. What's he up to now?' It was time to drive her to pick up her car from the garage where it was being repaired. On the way, I sought to further explain the inexplicable. We reached the garage and the mechanic presented me with the bill. 'Is that all it is?' I asked him. I wanted to pay him twice as much. I wanted to hug him (and he was not a hugger!); I loved him. I loved the whole world. What on earth was wrong with me? Nothing. I, the guilty one, who fully deserved to be condemned to hell, had been freely pardoned and was on my way to heaven. I understood grace in a way which I confess I am now tempted to forget. I loved all mankind and wanted all to be saved because I had the unshakeable conviction that God did. But over forty years have passed since that memorable day. If only I could feel that sense of grace and tenderness every time I stood to preach! Of course, I've not studied enough. Of course, I haven't prayed enough. Of course, my speech and delivery are pathetically inadequate. But the great truth that we often dry, sinful and needy preachers need to cling to is that we don't stand to preach from our pitifully shallow reservoirs, but from God's fresh, inexhaustible, ever-flowing river of grace and mercy. He can use frail people like you and me, all through the Holy Spirit's power. We shall see more of this later, but just now we need to probe a little more into not only *what* we are saying (the message) but *how* we are saying it (the manner) in order to be faithful ambassadors of the King and his word.

The God who feels ➡

Preaching that connects

IN THIS CHAPTER
Preaching from the heart, to the heart →
Preaching that hits the target →
Preaching that conveys the pathos of Scripture →

Chapter 4 ➡

David burned with anger against the man ... Then Nathan said to David, 'You are the man!'

–2 Sam. 12:5, 7

He spoke *from* the heart, and his words went *to* the heart.[1]

–Spoken of Bishop Hugh Latimer

I was visiting Northern Ireland and was booked to speak in a number of churches around the Province. Travelling to my next engagement I stopped for a break in a pleasant, small market town. Getting out of the car I heard what I thought was the sound of thunder, but soon discovered however that it was a man preaching to those who were browsing among the market stalls. His voice was booming through a speaker that looked as if it had been acquired from an eighties heavy metal band. Bizarrely, people were bustling about their business as though he were invisible and inaudible. I felt a strange mix of emotions at the sight of this spectacle. I love the gospel and making the Saviour known to those outside the church. I have a passion for open-air preaching. So what bugged me? The man evidently loved the gospel and cared for people. He was zealous and doctrinally sound from what I could hear of the message. But the great problem was, he was just not connecting with his 'target audience'. I will seek to speak to open-air preachers in the appendix at the back of the book, but for now, we will widen the matter to address all of us who seek to preach and teach. I am convinced it is an area in which many struggle—whether outside or inside a church building. Namely, how to connect with our hearers at the deepest level; with their emotions as well as their mind. Evangelist Roger Carswell said, 'We are to speak from the inmost passion of our heart, but to do so with winsome care, recognising that people have been wounded by the society in which they live, and blinded by the enemy of their souls.'[2] In these days of increasing uncertainty, never has there been such a need for us to preach with pathos-shaped wisdom. Additionally, many have had to grasp the challenge of speaking to people through a camera. So, with the absence of a live congregation and missing the interaction between preacher and people, the need for us to be moved by truth has never been greater.

Sound theology

Just to reiterate, I am taking for granted the fact that Scripture should be held in high regard. That said, there are many today hailed as 'great communicators', but sadly, their gift of connecting often comes at the expense of the truth. They are able to captivate their audience but there is a distinct lack of essential doctrinal content in their message, and at times—inexcusably—an omission of Christ and his all-important substitutionary work on the cross. But perhaps our challenge lies at the other end of the pendulum swing, namely we have sound doctrine in place but somehow have allowed ourselves to be hamstrung by it. We who have strong theological convictions need to be careful that we are not bound in a doctrinal straightjacket that restricts freedom and results in an overly-cautious kind of preaching. The outcome of that can be stiff, awkward and over-wordy sermon delivery. One gets the impression that some preachers live with a fear of uttering something 'unsound' which may lead to them being struck off a list of preachers they admire (imagined or real, living or dead). This restriction is the very opposite to the blessing a good grasp of theology should furnish us with. Doctrinal soundness should give our preaching wings not weights, speech that is free not frozen. Listen to a top jazz musician who soars and swings effortlessly, free as a bird. Or a rock guitar solo which seems to take off and reach heights previously unimagined. It didn't 'just happen'. Unseen, and unappreciated are hours, even years spent laboriously practicing scales and studying chord progressions. Then, having mastered them the artist is liberated and has abundant freedom to improvise, but within set boundaries. It is just like this for the preacher. Once we have sound doctrine in place, we are free to forget the 'framework' and soar. There will be a warmth, confidence and vibrancy about such a preacher. Martyn Lloyd-Jones said, 'Preaching is theology coming through a man who is on fire. A true understanding and experience of the Truth must lead to this.' We must endeavour to preach in a way that connects with our hearers, doing all within our powers to ensure our message hits the target. Veteran Bible teacher Jerry Vines says, 'Since the Bible pulsates with emotion, faithful exegetes will not only give attention to what the Bible text says, but also to how it says it.'[3]

Truth, emotion, connection

Approaching his adulterous and deceitful King, the prophet Nathan does not set out to just deliver the bare truth, 'You have committed adultery, murdered and lied! You have broken the commandments. Repent!' No, he wants his message to reach the very depths of David's heart in order to produce that 'godly sorrow that brings repentance' (2 Cor. 7:10). So, he skilfully unfolds (to a former shepherd!) a heart-breaking story of a rich man who cruelly steals a poor man's only possession, 'a little ewe lamb'. Burning with anger, David rages, 'this man deserves to die'. Nathan has his congregation on the ropes, so now comes in with the killer blow ... 'You are the man!' Boom! Truth, emotion and connection. In our preaching we have hard things to set before people at times—sin, judgment, everlasting punishment to name just three. How to most effectively communicate these subjects is a vital matter for us to wrestle with, and it remains a work in progress as situations and contexts constantly change. But we must be willing to work on it if we are aiming for real change in the lives of our hearers. Puritan Richard Sibbes says, 'It is not enough to have the heart broken, for a pot may be broken in pieces and yet be good for nothing; so may a heart be, through terrors, and a sense of judgment, and yet not be like wax, pliable. Therefore, it must be melted.' Many of us have read longingly of the impact preachers of past centuries enjoyed, and we seek to emulate them. But so often their pathos and warmth of appeal is lost in cold print. Reading Joseph Alleine's *Alarm to the Unconverted*, for example, you might be excused for thinking he was a mere tub-thumping, hell-fire preacher—the same might be said of Jonathan Edwards, George Whitefield, the Wesley brothers, Robert Murray M'Cheyne and a host of men God raised up to awaken past generations—but such was the pathos evident in these men's lives and voices, that hearts were melted and stubborn wills were brought into willing captivity to Jesus Christ. In most, if not all cases the message came from a tender, if not broken heart. Steven Lawson quotes George Whitefield's biographer, 'Fervent love lay at the very centre of Whitefield's effectiveness as an evangelist. As he preached, his love for sinners seemed to overpower them. "In all his discourses," John Gillies observes, "there was a fervent and melting love, an earnestness of persuasion, an outpouring of redundant love."'[4]

Fervent Love

It is impossible to give to others something we ourselves don't have. Perhaps one reason for a lack of 'fervent love' and pathos in our preaching could be that we struggle to believe that we ourselves really are loved by God. As a result, we live most of our spiritual lives under a cloud of heaviness. Very few of us live entirely free from a haunting sense of failure. Given enough room to move, this has the potential to debilitate, even paralyse, the most mature Christian. As preachers, we need often to preach to ourselves first. I have to remind myself often, it is God who first breathed new life into me and gave me these heavenly desires. Though it is my work to preach to others, I don't tire of reminding myself of the basic truths that bring comfort and assurance. Christians are those who rest and rejoice in the finished work of Jesus Christ accomplished for us on the cross. My comfort flows from the fact that 'he, himself bore our sins in his body on the tree' (1 Peter 2:24). My peace and joy therefore are dependent not on anything I could ever do for God, but entirely upon what he has done for me through the life, death and resurrection of his beloved Son. So, preach it dear brother! Speaking of the fruit of justification by faith, Paul states that, 'God's love has been poured out into our hearts through the Holy Spirit, who has been given to us' (Rom. 5:5). Robert Horn reminds us, 'God's love is always supernatural, always a miracle, and always the last thing we deserve.' But how hard it is for we saved but works-wired sinners to grasp the astounding 'free-ness' of grace, that we truly *have* been made saints and really *are* 'beloved children' as Paul writes (Eph. 3:1) One who tends towards legalism will be lacking as a preacher and consequently always have a hard edge to his preaching. He preaches the truth, but it comes over metallic and cold. In his introduction to *Gentle and Lowly*, Dan Ortland explains that he wrote his book, 'For those of us who know God loves us but suspect we have deeply disappointed Him.'[5] I am convinced that the greater our assurance of God's love for us, the more likely we are to speak of him to others as we ought—much as John Stott speaks of the 'indissoluble link between preacher and preaching'.[6] The man and the message are fused together as one. As preachers, we are called to communicate not through words alone but to *embody* the pathos of Scripture. Our body language, facial expressions, tone of voice will all be read and heard.

Tone of voice

I have already outlined the uniqueness and individuality of voice. If we are honest, though, we can sometimes be cast down by the limitations of our vocal equipment. Some seem to have a natural preaching voice that is strong, clear or melodic, whilst others of us have a weak, small voice that frustrates us because of its lack of power and penetration. A recognition and conviction of the sovereignty of God in the distribution of his gifts is of utmost importance here. It is interesting to note how both in Scripture and church history God places the right man in the right situation—despite the doubts his servants may have! There are times when our voice must bring healing and, at other times, awakening. It is no wonder that we may look with holy envy at a brother whose voice seems perfect to produce the effect we are seeking to achieve. We need to remember that God needs both a tender Richard Sibbes (nicknamed 'the Heavenly Doctor'), as well as a John Knox, the Reformer who 'lifted up his voice as a trumpet' and awakened Scotland. Reflecting on the brother preaching in the market in Northern Ireland, his main problem was not excessive volume but lack of pathos in his voice and perhaps, more seriously, a lack of empathy towards those he was seeking to reach. 'No man can be a great preacher without great feeling,' wrote James W. Alexander.

Mood

Our responsibility as exegetes is not merely to labour to convey *truth* but also to detect and then seek to communicate the *mood*, whether it be lament, rejoicing, anger, hope or whatever else. Having the sermon on paper, or in our mind is one thing, delivering it is another. This is why we are forced to cast ourselves constantly upon God in prayer. The first church we served was in the valleys of South Wales. Living next door to the Manse were a warm, good-humoured young couple who were not believers but showed interest in 'the work of the chapel'. Tony, a fanatical rugby player, learning that we met for prayer before each service chirped one day, 'I get it Mike, you go there to psyche yourself up before you preach!' Encouragingly, he had noted the necessity of our meeting for prayer before the service. But we are not 'method actors' employing a technique in order to give an emotionally expressive performance, but men reliant on the Spirit who inspired the passage to give us grace to convey the appropriate mood. We are to be so caught up in the truth, and so longing for it to bless our hearers that we express it naturally in our voice. The effect will be that our message will communicate at a deeper level than the cerebral as we engage the whole person in our preaching. 'Because the heart and mind are inseparable, we should unapologetically persuade both when we preach,' reasons Adam Dooley.[7] Let us look next then at the connection between heart and mind.

Heart and mind

IN THIS CHAPTER
The whole man in preaching →
The importance of persuasion in preaching →
The power of love in preaching →

Chapter 5

> … when they heard this, they were cut to the heart and said to Peter and the rest of the apostles, Brothers what should we do?
>
> –Acts 2:37

> What is preaching? Logic on fire! Eloquent reason!
>
> –Martyn Lloyd-Jones

As preachers of the word, we stand between two worlds; we are 'heralds of eternity in the courts of time'. In the light of such an awesome task and responsibility, we deeply desire to be faithful and effective communicators. To do this well, it is vital we hold the conviction that both heart and mind must be addressed. Again, this means paying attention to pathos as well as logos. Peter Mead says:

> The human is created as a more complex creature than a computer. We don't simply live from coding placed in our memory. We are heart-driven responders and relaters. We need to be informed. But in that informing process we ultimately need to encounter the Lord who reveals himself to us in His Word.[1]

All preaching should be edifying, but an increase in knowledge is not the end goal. Martin Lloyd Jones never tired of saying that preaching is not a lecture. 'I have often discouraged the taking of notes while I am preaching … The first and primary object of preaching is not only to give information. It is, as [Jonathan] Edwards says, to produce an impression... While you are writing your notes, you may be missing something of the impact of the Spirit.'[2] Lloyd-Jones, like Edwards two centuries before him, was engaged in fighting a battle on two fronts in his efforts to encourage preachers to address heart as well as the mind, emotions as well as the intellect. Jonathan Edwards, of course ministered in times of an extraordinary awakening and revival. On the one hand, he had to contend with those who dismissed the entire revival as mindless hysteria, whilst on the other he sought to correct those who seemed to think everything that happened in the revival was 'of God', no matter how weird or unbalanced it was. Lloyd-Jones, likewise, laboured to convince preachers they should not be content that the message preached is merely theologically 'sound' but that it comes with human warmth and passion and accompanied by divine power.

Our responsibility

With all the blessings that come from having firm views regarding God's sovereignty, such a conviction may at the same time place us in danger of stepping back from our responsibility, looking for God to do what he expects us to do. In the realm of evangelism, we know full well that we don't have the power to save or win anybody by our own means or devices, yet we see the Apostle Paul driving home our duty as preachers when he says, 'I have become all things to all people so that by all possible means I might save some' (1 Cor. 9:22). Yes, we are right to have concerns about taking the verse out of context as some have done—along with other verses like, 'He that wins souls is wise' (Prov. 11:30)—but any such fear is dispelled when we consider trustworthy Spurgeon's evangelistic classic, *The Soul Winner*. Passionate Calvinist (sadly, today too often an oxymoron!) Spurgeon laboured all through his years to stir God's people, and especially preachers, to their sacred duty in pleading with men and women. 'A sinner has a heart as well as a head; a sinner has emotions as well as thoughts; and we must appeal to both. A sinner will never be converted until his emotions are stirred ... Religion without emotion is religion without life.'[3] This kind of persuasive preaching is thoroughly biblical. When we consider the most fruitful message ever delivered— Peter's sermon on the Day of Pentecost—we note that it is Christ-centred, Spirit-empowered, full of Scripture, expository and extremely personal. We see clearly that the preacher was reluctant to finish without securing a response from the crowd, 'With many other words he warned them; and he pleaded with them, "Save yourselves from this corrupt generation"' (Acts 2:40). So, the question must be asked: why is there such an absence of heartfelt pleading in preaching today? There seems a distinct lack of what former generations called 'blood earnestness', an overflowing from the man's lips, the passion deep within his heart. It has often been said, 'Only what comes from the heart will reach the heart.' Again, we acknowledge the fact that we differ temperamentally and minister in a variety of situations and settings, but there is no excuse for lack of earnestness and urgency on our part as we preach eternal truths. Stuart Olyott states, 'Different preachers will express this in different ways and even the same preacher will express it in different ways on different occasions. But your urgency will come through.'[4]

Persuasion

The Judean King knew exactly what the man in the dock was attempting to do, and complained, 'Do you think that in such a short time you can persuade me to be a Christian?' (Acts 26:28). But we dare not think the necessity of earnestness applies only to evangelistic preaching. Persuasion is such an important element of pathos that it should course through all our preaching like the blood through our veins. Theodore Roosevelt's oft quoted statement, 'People don't care how much you know until they know how much you care,' has lost none of its power through overuse. It's a truth that we preachers, especially pastors, overlook at our peril. Without genuine love for people, preaching comes over as hollow and metallic. There can be no greater indictment then when one says, 'He loves preaching more than those to whom he preaches.' Converted slave trader, John Newton, advising a young man freshly entered into the ministry said, 'We cannot hope to be useful to our people, unless we give them reason to believe we love them, and have their interest at heart.'[5] Haranguing is not persuasion. Stuart Olyott again comments, 'Scolding is not usually the best method of persuading people to do something worthwhile ... Persuasion sets out to show people the suit you have tailored is worth wearing. It tells them of the happiness and blessedness that will come into their life if they put God's truth into practice.'[6] Notice the earnest, persuasive tone of the Apostle Paul when addressing the believers in the Galatian church. He writes, 'My dear children, for whom I am again in the pains of childbirth until Christ is formed in you ...' (Gal. 4:19). And then, when pleading with the saints in Corinth, 'So I will very gladly spend for you everything I have and expend myself as well. If I love you more, will you love me less?' (2 Cor. 12:15). Then note how frequently he uses the phrase, 'I beseech you' in his letters. He is not too embarrassed to plead, implore, even beg. Appeals from the heart will reach the heart. A man's preaching is powerful and persuasive because it is an overflow of the passion and pathos for people woven deeply into his soul. F. W. Boreham relates a story of an English pastor who sought to discover the secret for the powerful influence of Scottish pastor Robert Murray M'Cheyne. So not long after his death, he visited his church, St. Peter's in Dundee:

> The sexton, who had served under Mr. M'Cheyne, took the him into the vestry, and pointed to some of M'Cheyne's books still lying on the table. 'Sit down here,' said the old sexton, leading his visitor to the chair in which M'Cheyne used to sit. 'Now put your elbows on the table!' The visitor obeyed. 'Now put your face in your hands!' The visitor did so. 'Now let

the tears flow! That was the way Mr. McCheyne used to do!' The sexton then led his guest to the pulpit; and gave him a fresh series of instructions. 'Put your elbows down into the pulpit!' He put his elbows down. 'Now put you face in your hands!' He did so. 'Now let the tears flow! That was the way Mr. M'Cheyne used to do!'[7]

Geoff Thomas (who pastored the same church for over fifty years) challenges, 'Loving is absolutely indispensable for leaders in the church', and laments for those congregations who have to suffer listening to the loveless preacher on a regular basis, 'The Rev. Clanging Cymbal.' He continues, 'To be a pastor, the preacher must be in love with his people, and he must like people and be interested in them.'[8]

The power of love

Love is more than a divine attribute, it is the divine essence. Not that God *has* love, but that God *is* love. Love was one of the great motivating forces that drove Paul on unstoppably like a runaway locomotive preaching the word 'in season and out of season'. He was able to say, 'For Christ's love compels us, because we are convinced that one died for all, and therefore all died. And he died for all, that those who live should no longer live for themselves but for him who died for them and was raised again' (2 Cor. 5:14–15). Calvary love flowed out of him and into others. Perhaps our greatest need is to receive a revelation of the immeasurable

Heart and mind

love that Paul speaks of and prays the believers in Ephesus might receive (Eph. 3:18–19). Most Christians will be familiar with Dwight Lyman Moody, the influential American evangelist who lived during the latter part of the nineteenth century. Not so many will have heard of Henry Moorhouse an English Methodist preacher, but Moody was never the same following his encounter with this young man. Roger Carswell describes the moment:

> The best-known evangelist of that day was the American, D. L. Moody. Henry Moorhouse met Moody when as a young man he was preaching in England. Moorhouse introduced himself by saying, 'I'll preach for you in America!' Moody politely but rashly said, 'If you should ever get to Chicago, come down to my church and I will give you a chance to preach.' Months later Moorhouse followed this through, telegramming Moody to say he was in Chicago. Moody had to be true to his promise, so reluctantly agreed for Moorhouse to preach when he himself was away. Upon his return Moody asked his wife how the young preacher did. 'Oh, he is a better preacher than you are,' his wife said. 'He is telling sinners that God loves them.' 'That is not right,' said Moody. 'God does not love sinners.' 'Well,' she said, 'you go and hear him. He has been preaching all week, and he has only had one verse for a text. It is John 3:16.' Moody went, and heard Henry Moorhouse preach on that one verse and afterward said it was on

Preaching the Heart of God

that night that he first clearly understood the gospel and God's great love. Now, instead of only preaching that God is going to judge sinners, so people should flee from the wrath to come, Moody could preach God's great demonstration of love, that Jesus died, taking on himself the sin that would condemn us and offering forgiveness and new life. Moody said, 'I have never forgotten those nights hearing Henry Moorhouse. I have preached a different gospel since, and I have had more power with God and men since then.'[9]

Isn't this what *all* preachers crave? More power with God and man! 'If you can really make a man believe you love him, you have won him,' Moody would later say. He was radically transformed by coming to see the importance of pathos. He was then able to put it into action in the kind of preaching that could melt the hardest of hearts.

Heart and mind →

Hard truths and melting words

IN THIS CHAPTER
The incarnate God our pattern →
The preacher and the Hyper-Calvinism trap →
The preacher and his vulnerability →

Chapter 6 ➡

Whoever believes in the Son has eternal life, but whoever rejects the Son will not see life, for God's wrath remains on them.

–John 3:36

It's not saying hard things that pierces the conscience ... it is the voice of divine love among the thunder.[1]

–Andrew A. Bonar

In the early eighties, theologian F.F. Bruce wrote *The Hard Sayings of Jesus*, a book dealing helpfully with some (seventy!) of the Saviour's difficult teachings—the title being taken from a phrase found in the sixth chapter of John's Gospel. After Jesus' bread of life discourse in John 6, a number of professed disciples of Christ stopped following him because they were offended by what they dubbed his 'hard sayings' (John 6:60–65). Nothing has changed in over 2000 years. It is a fact we have to live with that there will always be those who baulk at certain truths we preach from Scripture. From cover to cover, the Bible contains things which will undoubtedly cause offence, and the temptation to avoid any 'difficult' passages or 'harsh' doctrines is always with us, and is to be resisted with all our might. While this may not be one of those areas in which we struggle, our temptation is to look down our noses at those preachers who we feel pander to the crowd and fawn over the throng who gather to hear their 'candy-coated homilies'. We, on the other hand see ourselves among the sound and the strong, the faithful ones who unflinchingly hold firm convictions. We believe with all our might that without a saving faith in Jesus Christ all are lost and heading unprepared for judgement and then to hell—for ever. We 'Amen!' articles, books and papers that defend these robust and essential biblical doctrines and would 'go to war' against those who soft peddle them. And rightly so. But somehow their solemn truths don't seem to have reached our hearts and affected us as they ought. For the Apostle Paul, and many of our 'heroes' throughout Church history, these 'hard truths' did, and they appeared to produce a twofold fruit—emotion and action. 'Therefore, knowing the fear of the Lord, we persuade others,' writes Paul (2 Cor. 5:11).

Awe and tenderness

We should be afraid to preach on hell. Not out of cowardice, but simply because it is beyond our ability to speak of it with sufficient awe and tenderness. Robert M'Cheyne, meeting up with his closest friend Andrew Bonar one Monday, inquired what Bonar had preached on the previous day, only to receive the answer, 'Hell.'

M'Cheyne asked searchingly, 'Did you preach it with tears?'[2] If you read through M'Cheyne's sermons you will detect that his preaching was clearly in line with the faith of the Reformers and Puritans. He never flinched from preaching 'hard truths', searchingly. Yet again, we must say, cold print fails to convey the trembling throb of pathos and tenderness that accompanied his words. This is true of all the men we read who have stood like lofty peaks in the mountain range of preachers through the centuries in their efforts to awaken a slumbering world to the reality of eternity and the wrath to come. Written sermons of the Puritans, Whitefield, Wesley, Spurgeon and the like can never communicate to us the warmth of pathos and compassion that filled their hearts then fell from their lips. Like their Saviour, they were not dry-eyed, emotionally stifled men.

Pathos Incarnate

Our supreme pattern when it comes to pathos, of course has to be the incarnate God, Jesus Christ, the very embodiment of pathos. The entire life of the 'man of sorrows' was punctuated by words and deeds of overflowing compassion. At the tomb of his friend, 'he was deeply moved in his spirit and greatly troubled' (John 11:33). His humanity was so moved that 'He wept' ... literally, 'burst into tears' (John 11:35). It was then that he immediately spoke with divine authority that raised his decomposing friend from the tomb. We see him gazing upon the multitudes and are told that '... he had compassion on them, because they were like sheep without a shepherd. *So, he began teaching them many things*' (Mark 6:34). His speech flowed from a heart that was moved. Of great significance is the reaction of the hard-bitten temple guards, who when sent by the religious leaders to arrest Jesus, return empty handed and report in breathless bewilderment, 'No one ever spoke the way this man does' (John 7:46). And then, we picture him looking down upon a doomed Jerusalem, where once again we are told, he 'wept'. Speaking of the Saviour's sorrow over Jerusalem, Presbyterian pastor and author Maurice Roberts writes, 'In the heart of Christ, there is a deep holy instinct, a desire to save everybody, everywhere. There is that instinct within him whereby he was activated by desire even for those that hated him, even for the worst of men, even those he knew would never believe, yet his overtures of compassion were extended to them.'[3]

Joy

But let us not for a moment think of Christ as morose. Pathos was evident not only in his sorrow, but also in the joy that filled his heart. Donald MacLeod states, 'A joyless life would have been a sinful life. Jesus experienced deep, habitual joy.'[4] One of the great Messianic psalms speaks of this:

> You love righteousness and hate wickedness;
> > therefore God, your God, has set you above your companions
> > by anointing you with the oil of *joy*. (Psalm 45:7)

Spurgeon, preaching on the subject of our Saviour's joy and the effect it would have upon others says, 'I fully believe that there was never on the face of the earth a man who knew so profound and true a gladness as our blessed Lord. Did he not desire that his joy might be in his people that their joy might be full?'[5] The preacher is not a machine. Neither is he a super-man who is above having to fight to maintain joy in the midst of life's struggles. God has chosen to communicate his truth through frail human vehicles. We are men who can be downcast, fearful, insecure, temperamental and subject to the very trials and temptations experienced by those listening to us. However, we should see these struggles and experiences as friends to our ministry, not foes. Although always unwelcome, they are vital, simply because they equip and enable us to identify with the trials and tribulations of those to whom we preach. They also help to relieve our listeners from having the additional burden of having to endure hollow sermons from a shallow preacher.

Identification

We must not be too embarrassed nor too proud to admit to our hearers that we have exactly the same struggles to contend with as them. Surely there is not a more tragic sight than a man who gives the impression when he is preaching that he is of an altogether different breed to those to whom he preaches and condescendingly addresses his hearers from his elevated position. Speaking of this problem, Stuart Olyott says:

> How many times have you witnessed the following scenario? Jack Jones of modest roots has come from total obscurity to train for the ministry. When his period of study is over he is duly ordained and

begins his first pastorate. At this moment a great change comes over him: Jack Jones from Nowhere in the county of Nothingness begins to behave as if he were a member of a superior caste who has little in common with the lesser mortals who surround him.[6]

How different it is with the man who was God. And how blessed we sinners are because of it. 'For we do not have a high priest who is unable to empathise with our weaknesses, but we have one who has been tempted in every way, just as we are—yet he did not sin' (Heb. 4:15). Although we are told that 'He had no beauty or majesty to attract us to him, nothing in his appearance that we should desire him' (Isa. 53:2), there is an incredible inner beauty in Jesus that enlightened eyes can see and Spirit-touched hearts can feel. He is our supreme pattern when it comes to pathos in preaching, whether it be in rebuke, encouragement or invitation. Christ, who is 'the image of the invisible God' (Col. 1:15) is the very heart of God revealed in its purest and most accessible form. It is our duty and privilege to preach him at all times, and when not preaching him directly, to preach in the spirit of Christ. Ortland describes him as having, 'a heart that upbraids the impenitent with all the harshness that is appropriate, yet embraces the penitent with more openness that we are able to feel'.[7] Perhaps at times, we underestimate the power of the truth we handle and seek to supplement it by an unnecessary sternness in our tone. Derek Bingham encourages us, 'Gentle words fall lightly, but have great weight.'[8]

Love for *all* sinners?

There can often exist, lurking in the deep, inner recesses of our hearts, a dark and icy nook where harsh thoughts reside, and on occasions burst forth from our lips like a thunder clap. In our determination not to compromise God's holiness and uphold his disdain for sin, we may struggle to grasp that divine grace which pities and loves all indiscriminately, even the worst of sinners. Without doubt, the love of God for his elect, those who alone benefit from the saving work of Christ, is unique and distinct from all other loves. Robert Sheehan was a Reformed pastor and author of exceptionally sharp intellect whose ministry in his short life was greatly esteemed by the wider church. Seeking to protect from any subtle intrusion of a cold, hyper-Calvinistic aloofness in our thinking and preaching, he challenged us with these words, 'As Jesus preached and healed all sorts of people, some who would believe and some who would not, the elect and the non-elect, he had compassion towards them because they were like sheep without a shepherd' (Matthew 9:36). He did not look at the crowd with a distinguishing squint, with compassion on the elect but not on the non-elect! He had compassion on the crowd universally and promiscuously. This compassion to all, which so marked his words, was a regular feature of his ministry.' Here is God incarnate, who by his words and actions plainly demonstrated a love for all who stood before him. Sheehan continues, 'Our Lord exhorted his disciples to love their enemies and do them good, not only because their reward would be great but also because by so doing they would be sons of the Most High, because He is kind to the unthankful and evil (Luke 6:35). We are to love our enemies because God loves His. His mercy is the pattern for ours.'[9] Iain H. Murray records how hyper-Calvinism was one of the first controversies in which the young Spurgeon engaged when he began preaching in London at the age of just nineteen. 'No one listening to Spurgeon could be left in any doubt that God is not willing that any should perish', writes Murray concerning the earnest, warm and tender pleading Spurgeon demonstrated throughout his entire life and ministry.[10] It would be good to ask the reason why there seems so little evidence of this solemn yet deeply affectionate pleading with the unsaved in our preaching today. Why is it that so many sermons are delivered in such a 'take it or leave it' manner?

Hard truths and melting words

The most powerful and effective preachers have been those who have sought to faithfully preach 'the whole counsel of God', holding nothing back of those 'hard truths' that must be made known, and yet doing so with Christ-like pathos and affection. Gideon Ouseley (1762–1839) had the task of preaching the gospel in Ireland at a time when the majority of the population held the staunch conviction they must 'live and die Roman Catholics'. Gospel preachers were furiously opposed and had to endure all kinds of physical attacks. But it was said of him, 'In his preaching of both law and gospel, love was expressed in his every tone and movement, and could not fail to make an impression on their hearts.' After his death, one who had witnessed his labours wrote, 'I see him now ... his gestures, his fire, his pathos, his smile, his benignity, his powerful persuasiveness and tact.' Ouseley's biographer, speaking of his Christ-likeness writes, 'The love of God was in him and shone through him. His pity for others was part of his love for Christ which he enjoyed.'[11]

A fragrance

Being convinced that it is the preacher's responsibility to convey the truth in more than words, means that we will have the conviction that our lives will either add to or subtract from the message we seek to communicate. We cannot be neutral in this respect. The Apostle Paul says that 'we are to God the pleasing aroma of Christ among those who are being saved and among those who are perishing' (2 Cor. 2:15). In other words, the fragrance of our lives is pleasing to God, but it also attracts others to him ... or repels them. Smells are powerful in attracting (a beautiful perfume) or repelling (a sewer!), and are difficult to ignore. In the days of the Roman Empire, after a major victory in battle it was customary to celebrate before the citizens of Rome with magnificent parades. As a part of the ceremonies, fragrances and incense would be burned throughout the city as the armies marched through to the sound of triumphant music and the sweet aroma of victory.

Even those who did not attend the parade could hear the music and smell the sweet aroma and knew that Rome had been victorious. Paul speaks of Christians 'spreading everywhere the fragrance of the knowledge' of their precious Saviour.

Crushed

We said at the beginning that preaching that comes with the pathos that a broken world longs for comes at a cost. This spiritual fragrance is spread only when, like certain flowers, there is a crushing process. Amy Carmichael, in her poem 'Hast Thou No Scar', touchingly highlights the inevitability of wounds and scars for all who seek to follow in the Master's footsteps, whilst at the same time exposing the folly of seeking to minister without this inescapable brokenness:

> Hast thou no scar?
> No hidden scar on foot, or side, or hand?
> I hear thee sung as mighty in the land;
> I hear them hail thy bright, ascendant star.
> Hast thou no scar?
>
> Hast thou no wound?
> Yet I was wounded by the archers; spent,
> Leaned Me against a tree to die; and rent
> By ravening beasts that compassed Me, I swooned.
> Hast thou no wound?

> No wound? No scar?
> Yet, as the Master shall the servant be,
> And piercèd are the feet that follow Me.
> But thine are whole; can he have followed far
> Who has nor wound nor scar?[12]

John Newton, who knew what it was to pass through 'many dangers, toils and snares', testifies, 'My grand point in preaching is to break the hard heart, and to heal the broken one.' To accomplish this is a virtually impossible task, were it not for divine help promised. We should note the secret of Gideon Ouseley's effectiveness as a preacher, 'The love of God was in him and shone through him.' This surely is preaching at its finest, when a flawed, feeble man brings the 'loaves and fishes' of his life to the one who then gives heaven's touch. Our comfort ultimately rests in the grace and power of the Holy Spirit who is available to all who come with the conviction that without him we can do nothing of eternal significance.

Pathos and the Spirit

IN THIS CHAPTER
The glorious unpredictability of preaching →
The Spirit's unction and preaching →
The preacher's trials that convert to power →

Chapter 7 ➡

My message and my preaching were not with persuasive words of wisdom, but with a demonstration of the Spirit's power.

–1 Cor. 2:4

As he spoke, heaven came to earth. Another Voice was heard. The invisible world was more real than the visible one. There was a touch of glory ... the congregation sat in stunned silence overcome by the sheer power of the word.[1]

–Stuart Olyott speaking about Hywel Griffiths

The 'romance' of preaching

Observe a swan as it waddles awkwardly around, ungainly, flat-footed, tight-hipped. Yet, something incredible happens when it takes to the water. It smoothly and gracefully glides away and seems a different creature altogether. Is there not a similar transformation experienced by a preacher at times? Like every other Christian, a preacher is simply a lost cause who has been rescued and redeemed by the incomparable Christ. We are only too aware of our weaknesses, varying moods and perpetual unworthiness. If only we were employed as actors, or even politicians we could deliver our lines, leave and be satisfied the job is done. But, to quote Pitt-Watson again, 'Unless there is some measure of emotional involvement on the part of the preacher and on the part of his hearers the *kerygma* cannot be heard in its fullness.'[2] To restate: the man and his message are indivisibly and interdependently one. And yet, despite the constant awareness of his unfitness for such a high calling, there are those times when he is conscious that it is for this very purpose he has been born. What has made the difference? The Holy Spirit. Somehow the hours of sweat and struggle that eventually morphed into a pitiful sermon on a bit of paper has sprung into life and he finds himself—preacher and hearers—lifted to a higher dimension. As Martyn Lloyd-Jones explains at such times, there is:

> ... clarity of thought, clarity of speech, ease of utterance, a great sense of authority and confidence as you are preaching, an awareness of power not your own thrilling through the whole of your being, and an indescribable sense of joy. You are a man 'possessed', you are taken hold of, and taken up. I like to put it like this—and I know of nothing on earth that is comparable to this feeling—that when this happens you have a feeling that you are not actually doing the preaching, you are looking on at yourself in amazement as this is happening. It is not your effort; you are just an instrument, the channel, the vehicle: the Spirit is using you, and you are looking on in great enjoyment and astonishment.[3]

A slave to feelings

If only that could be our experience every time we open our mouths to speak. But this is why we speak of the 'romance' in preaching, because it is completely beyond our ability to predict and control. The manipulators, of course have no such problem, they will *make* it happen! But it is having a 'bad Sunday' that is helpful for two reasons: 1) We appreciate the 'good' Sundays. 2) We are reminded that it is God who makes the difference. Have you ever had the experience of feeling 'on top of the world' yet when it came to the preaching all was struggle from start to finish? Conversely, you are just not up to it, perhaps because of some upsetting news, or a heavy cold, the car has broken down on the way to church, or you have barked at the kids. You feel a hypocrite now even attempting to speak to others of the precious truths you have prepared and are called to deliver. But then something happens. You are quickened. You come alive. And suddenly all your earthly traumas and defects are forgotten. Your eyes are off yourself and your concerns and you are taken up with heavenly, eternal things. The lesson is, forget your feelings. They are no indicator of how you will communicate God's word. Any blessing upon a ministry is entirely of grace. Not that it relieves us of the duty and responsibility of prayer and preparation, seeking God for his presence and blessing on our efforts. But, at the end of the day, we want people to go away with an impression of *him*, not ourselves or our sermons.

Unction

So, first of all, we are ordinary men, seeking to preach with a pathos which flows from our God-given human emotions. Then there is that something additional which only God can give, and just for that particular occasion. What is it then? This 'extra' or 'unction' the great preachers of old would speak about and long for? That mysterious influence which brings a heavenly pathos upon the message our best efforts could never produce? E.M Bounds, wrestling to define it, says:

> It is that indefinable, indescribable something which an old, renowned Scottish preacher describes thus: 'There is sometimes somewhat in preaching that cannot be ascribed either to matter or expression, and cannot be described what it is, or from whence it cometh, but with a sweet violence it pierces into the heart and affections and comes immediately from the Word; but if there be any way to obtain such a thing, it is by the heavenly disposition of the speaker.'[4]

Stuart Olyott, recalling the impact the preaching of Hywel Griffiths had upon him whilst a theological student in his early-twenties wrote, 'As he spoke, heaven came to earth.' Significantly, Stuart's mother, in seeking to persuade her young son on his visit home in West Wales to hear this elderly former miner said, 'There was something about Hywel that could not be put into words,' but that he would 'understand if he could hear him for himself.' Stuart says that he was never the same after those times of sitting under his powerful preaching and points to three significant elements: 1) He clearly felt the truths he was preaching. 2) He poured out his love for everyone present. 3) Accompanying all he said there was an indefinable influence.[5]

Time and trials

We must ever be aware that preaching is not the product of so many hours in the study, but the overflow of a consecrated life. 'Out *of the overflow* of the *heart*, the *mouth speaks', taught he who was* anointed with the Holy Spirit and with power *(Mark 6:45; Acts 10:38)*. E.M. Bounds argued that it takes twenty years to produce a sermon because it takes twenty years to produce the man.[6] God is never in a hurry and through the years, in stress and sickness, trial and temptation, sorrow and joy, he is patiently shaping, moulding and preparing his instrument. There is always a cost in gaining and then keeping a tender heart. How many I wonder would be willing to pay the price and pray, 'Lord, use me... *whatever the cost'*? Many perhaps dream of having the gifts and influence of a Spurgeon, but few would desire his prolonged years of suffering. Michael Reeves writes:

> From the age of thirty-three, physical pain became a large and constant feature of life for him. He suffered from a burning kidney inflammation called Bright's Disease, as well as gout, rheumatism, and neuritis. The pain was such that it soon kept him from preaching for one-third of the time. Added to that,

overwork, stress, and guilt about the stress began to take their toll ... today he would almost certainly be diagnosed as clinically depressed and treated with medication and therapy.[7]

However, few outstripped Spurgeon in humour, cheerfulness ... and Spirit-filled pathos. One observer of his preaching noted, 'It is in pathos he excels, though he does not seem aware of it,' and another, 'His pathos brought tears to all eyes.'[8] We want pathos. We want the Spirit. But are we empty, humble and desperate enough to be filled? Once isn't enough. Twice isn't enough. We must come back again and again, Oliver-like with our little empty bowls, convinced that the greatest need of our hearers is for us to decrease and the Lord in us to increase. Bounds again says, 'The constraining power of love must be in the preacher as a projecting, eccentric, all-commanding, self-oblivious force.'[9] It is the Holy Spirit who gives that extra dimension to our words so they come clothed with a heavenly pathos, giving preaching what Lloyd-Jones called, a 'melting quality'. But there can be no melting without heat.

Pathos and the Spirit

Heat and light

IN THIS CHAPTER

The preacher and genuine earnestness →
The preacher and the power of kindness →
The preacher and 'natural' spirituality →

Chapter 8

> He was a burning and a shining light ...
> –John 5:35 KJV

> Light without heat never affects anybody. Heat without light is no good. You must have light and heat.[1]
> –Martyn Lloyd-Jones

The Lord Jesus pointed out something of great significance in the ministry of John the Baptist when speaking of him as 'a burning and shining light'. No one could ignore his preaching. He came on a mission not just to inform but to enflame. His concern was not merely that minds would be fed but that passions might be fuelled. It was not the length of the message he brought but the depth of feeling behind it. Could it be that we are so fearful in our times of being labelled 'anti-intellectual' that we are content to merely deliver truth, satisfied then that our work is done? John Murray, the late professor of Westminster Seminary in Philadelphia and one of the leading theologians of the twentieth century was once asked, 'What is the difference between a lecture and preaching?' He responded, 'Preaching is a personal, passionate plea.'[2] In all our legitimate endeavours to be contemporary heralds to our generation, one of those 'must haves' is the penetrating power of pathos. Bruce Bickel reminds us of our rich preaching heritage when speaking of our forebears, 'The Puritan's concern was light and heat—light from the pure Word of God to penetrate the darkness of the heart and soul of the hearer, heat from the pathos and passion of the heart and soul of the preacher to bring about conviction.'[3] It is our duty to leave our hearers in no doubt that, whatever they may think about the content of our message, we are in earnest and that we at least believe the things we speak about.

Earnestness

Appealing for earnestness in our communication of truth, John Stott wrote, 'Earnestness is deep feeling, and is indispensable to preachers.' He then quotes James W. Alexander of Princeton, 'It is a matter of universal observation that a speaker who would excite deep feeling must feel deeply himself.'[4] Once again, it must be emphasised, this is nothing to do with our temperament, upbringing or education—these things may help or hinder. What really matters is a man coming fresh from the presence of God, with the Word of God, in the power of God; ethos, logos and pathos yoked powerfully together as one in the service of the King. We must resist the temptation of thinking good exegesis and exposition of Scripture is sufficient. John MacArthur appeals for truth faithfully exegeted to then be conveyed with earnestness, 'The conscientious preacher does not merely seek to impart abstract doctrine or plain facts to his people; he also pleads with them for heartfelt obedience.'[5] MacArthur's words cause us to ask the question, 'What place do we give to the importance of pleading and persuading in our preaching?'

But this the twenty-first century!

There seems to be the fear currently that any display of earnestness today is 'uncool' and causes our message to sound dated. Thankfully the unnatural 'pulpit voice' that afflicted previous generations of preachers is disappearing, and we see a return to a more natural delivery. But it is that pendulum problem again, as we notice a burgeoning swing towards a detached, dispassionate delivery style. Perhaps it is because of concern over our postmodern hearers' rejection of absolute truth and disdain of authoritarianism. Aware of this we tread cautiously, not wanting to be seen as being pressurising or assertive. But ironically, we address a 'touchy-feely' generation that can cope with emotion and in these days of bland relativism long for a voice of authority, yet accompanied by empathy and compassion. Dr. Jeffrey Arthurs, Professor of Preaching and Communication at Gordon-Conwell Theological Seminary writes, 'Postmoderns desire an experience of reality, not statements about it.' He then adds, 'Unfortunately, most of our training equips us to exegete and communicate the ideas of the text, not the feelings.'[6] Significantly, those we perhaps patronizingly pigeon-hole 'Gen Z' (loosely, people born from 1995 to 2010) are not embarrassed to show passion and emotion when engaged in a cause worth fighting for. In fact they are suspicious of those who say they believe something passionately and yet fail to show it. (This perhaps explains why we get such a hearing from the younger generation when speaking on the streets. They do not appear at all 'put off' by the gospel being taken to the streets as many Christians would have us believe.) From the cradle they have been subject to an aggressive atheistic evolutionary 'gospel' that preaches that humans are merely a random bag of chemicals, made for no real purpose in life, have no real worth, and as a consequence, have no real hope. Having been robbed of an education that teaches them they are a unique 'one off'—created by a loving, personal Creator, made in his image and of infinite eternal worth—there is, not surprisingly, a response when someone comes to them warmly with a revolutionary message which blows out of the water all they have been taught!

Kindness

We are living in days of bitter division in almost every area of life. Just spending the shortest time on social media, you are struck by just how cutting, caustic and unkind we can be to each other. It is not simply the fact we disagree, but there is a venomous manner in which we show our disagreement. Appallingly, we witness cold hearts overflowing with unkind words, even from the lips (or fingertips) of God's people. And dare we say it, even from those whose work is to stand and speak on behalf of the God of all grace. We spoke earlier of the power of love in our preaching, but in considering the matter of 'heat' we must not underestimate the melting power of kindness. God is incredibly kind. I think we preachers need constant reminders that it is his kindness that is most powerful in producing repentance. Paul seems to be doing this when writing to the Christians in Rome, 'Do you presume on the riches of his kindness and forbearance and patience, not knowing that God's *kindness* is meant to lead you to repentance?' (Rom. 2:4). Kindness seems to penetrate the armour where all other weapons simply bounce off. Rosaria Butterfield was an intelligent, radical, staunch unbeliever, a lesbian utterly scornful of Christianity. After publishing a critique of a local evangelical group of Christians in a newspaper article, she received a mailbag full of response, much of it hurtful and hateful. But among the mail was a letter from a local pastor. 'It was a kind and inquiring letter,' she says. 'It had a warmth and civility to it, in addition to its probing questions ... Its tone demonstrated that the writer wasn't against her.' She reflected later, 'It was the kindest letter of opposition I had ever received.' They met and her friendship with the pastor and his wife led to her faith in Christ. The pastor knew the importance of communicating heat as well as light, flesh and blood emotion with eternal truth. Pathos as well as logos.

Restoring grace

Whether preaching to 'on the run' sinners or those who are 'returned and redeemed', all stand in need of the Lord's lavish, restoring grace. They come before us expectantly each week, battered, bruised and broken in some way by this world and in need of his healing touch. Wounds can be deep. Traumatic memories can be pushed down deep below the surface and mere human words totally inadequate in reaching them. Fanny Crosby in her inspiring hymn reminds us:

> Down in the human heart, crushed by the tempter.
> Feelings lie buried that grace can restore;
> Touched by a loving heart, wakened by kindness.
> Chords that were broken will vibrate once more.[7]

Comforting the disturbed and disturbing the comfortable is no easy task. Our preaching must have that penetrating quality which has power to both wound and heal, convict and encourage, tear down and build up—and all at the same time. This, of course, is humanly impossible. It is the Holy Spirit alone, working in and through the preacher who can accomplish this. Speaking of this divine enabling again, E.M. Bounds says:

It is the sweetest exhalation of the Holy Spirit. It impregnates, suffuses, softens, percolates, cuts and soothes. It carries the Word like dynamite, like salt, like sugar; makes the Word a soother, an accuser, a revealer, a searcher; makes the hearer a culprit or a saint, makes him weep like a child and live like a saint ...[8]

Our hearers need to be 'touched by a loving heart' and 'wakened by kindness'. So, what can we do in order to play our part in being conveyors of such grace to people, some of whom we may even struggle to like?

Time alone with God

For a preacher, the nearest we get to tasting heaven is the

awareness that there is something flowing from our heart and lips that is way beyond what we ourselves are capable of. It is when there is the absence of this—the painful realisation that all is so mechanical and we sound like a babbling dummy—that we are forced to retreat in private and beg the Lord not to leave us to our own resources again. Having others pray for us is good, but it is no substitute to being alone with God. It is alone, in private fellowship with him where our proud hearts are humbled, and our hardened hearts are made tender. But how difficult it is to pray. The flesh shrinks from it and we would do anything rather than 'be still'. Prayer rarely feels 'powerful' when we are engaged in it. Although there may be those precious times of liberty in prayer, it mostly seems just so 'ordinary'. But prayer honours God, and God honours prayer. When we pray, we are saying, 'God I believe in you.' So, we just take the Lord at his word and pray! 'Ask and it will be given to you; seek and you will find; knock and the door will be opened to you. For everyone who asks receives; the one who seeks finds; and to the one who knocks, the door will be opened' (Matt. 7:7–8). We must not wait until we *feel* like praying—just pray! One old prayer warrior, Moody Stuart, gave this advice, '1) Pray until you pray. 2) Pray until you are conscious of being heard. 3) Pray until you receive an answer.'[9] The point is we will rarely feel like praying. Pray anyway. When we do pray, the mind often flits and flutters and we struggle to get into a spirit of prayer. But keep on praying, it is not in vain. Beside praying to receive answers, 'Prayer freshens the heart of the preacher, keeps it in tune with God, and in sympathy with the people', encourages Bounds.[10] Remember, it's not so much the length, but the quality of time spent in prayer that matters. What counts is the depth and richness upon a life that is spent with God, therefore the reason for the Apostle Paul's directive to 'Pray without ceasing'. Throughout each day we will naturally lift up our hearts in thankfulness, seek his wisdom when we are unsure about something or cry out when we are afraid or in need. It is the dependency and comfort a child enjoys with a parent who loves and cares for them. At all times, we must aim to be 'natural in our spiritual life and spiritual in our natural life'. There is no dichotomy between the two realms.

Family life

There was a time when the idea of being a preacher was the furthest thought from our minds. Many of us were far from God, and happy to be so. But the day of days dawned when we 'came to our senses' and humbly acknowledged our need and received free forgiveness for every act of rebellion against our Maker. As if it were not enough to be cleansed and acquitted of every sin, we were lovingly 'taken home' and adopted into his family. Incredible! Whether heavenly or earthly, the family is God's idea. Foolishly, when the pressure is on, we can fall into the temptation of viewing our earthly family as just another tick on our 'to do' list instead of being at the top of our agenda. Besides using the 'cut and thrust' of family life to shape and mould us,

Heat and light ➡

God has a way of keeping our hearts tender through all the joys and sorrows, trials and triumphs that we pass through together. Those with a 'prodigal' in the family will know this especially. May we never forget that God has chosen to reveal himself to us as 'Father'.

> No earthly father loves like Thee,
> No mother half so mild
> Bears and forbears, as Thou hast done
> With me, thy sinful child.[11]

Warm, mature believers

Let us forever guard against drifting into that pietistic loner mentality which can lead to a cool aloofness, an inability to relate to others in a natural way, and even a reluctance to accept correction or criticism. We must use every means that providence has placed within our reach to deepen, grow and develop—especially in this area of pathos. Of course, growth in godliness is a life-long practice and God has graciously and generously gifted his church with those from whom we can learn; and pride must not hinder us from receiving. We who are teachers must be humble and teachable. So, seek out those who are warm, mature and spiritually-minded. Read the writings of those who have walked closely with God. Listen to preachers who have that ability not just to feed the mind but stir the soul.

'Fire' books

Writing from prison, his days numbered, the aged apostle

seeks to prepare young preacher and pastor Timothy for the rigors of ministry that awaited him. Poignantly he urges, 'fan into flame the gift of God, which is in you' (2 Tim. 1:6). Keeping the flame alive is surely the duty of each of us called to 'Preach the word ... in season, out of season' (2 Tim. 4:2). Addressing a group of young Salvation Army officers, 'General' William Booth said (perhaps even barked), 'I want you young men always to bear in mind that it is the nature of fire to go out; you must keep it stirred and fed, and the ashes removed.'[12] Whilst still a fairly new Christian at Bible College, I felt the need to do something to counteract the intake of information I was struggling to absorb. Wonderful though it all was, and as deeply grateful as I felt receiving such rich spiritual fare from a gifted and godly faculty, I sensed I was in danger of forgetting the very purpose for which I was there. So, I had a shelf in my rapidly growing library dedicated to what I named my 'fire books'. Certain books and authors I would turn to if feeling dry or down and in need of perspective. I knew that I could open any one of them, almost at random and within minutes they had the ability to 'fan into flame' my dulling heart and jaded spirit. I have continued this practice through the years up to this very day. It has been a life-safer, especially through busy and pressurised days of ministry. The collection has enlarged, of course, but among them are those precious early 'fire books' the Holy Spirit first used to call me into this glorious work.

Heat and light

Giving out to others

It is in giving out that we receive. Perhaps you have experienced times when a spirit of heaviness or depression was relieved by reaching out to help someone in need. Despite that foot-dragging reluctance, you phoned someone to encourage them, or shared your faith, or wrote a card. Somehow you were released. The darkness fled and joy and warmth filled your heart. It is simply the joy of obedience. It's not rocket science. Love God, love others—even when you don't feel like it. 'I'm going to love everybody, even if it kills me,' vowed a determined A.W. Tozer. Fresh acts of repentance, loving deeds of faith are the way to 'keep a clear conscience before God and man' (Acts 24:16) and keep us in the right place allowing us to be clear channels through which pathos can freely flow.

A heart after God's own

IN THIS CHAPTER
A heart in tune with God →
A consistent child-like humility →
A pathos-shaped ministry →

Epilogue

> I have found David son of Jesse, a man after my own heart.
>
> —Acts 13:22

> The preacher ... must go forth as a man among men, clothed with humility, abiding in meekness, wise as a serpent, harmless as a dove; the bonds of a servant with the spirit of a king, a king in high, royal, in dependent bearing, with the simplicity and sweetness of a child.[1]
>
> —E.M. Bounds

Despite the glaring faults and failures in the life of David, Israel's King, we are told that he was 'a man after God's own heart' (1 Samuel 13:14; Acts 13:22). If we are men aspiring to preach the heart of God, we must strive to be those who have something of his heartbeat within us. To understand what a heart after God's own looks like, then we need only to consider the Psalms that flowed from David's lips and pen. In so many of the Psalms we see the 'cry of the soul' expressed in such beauty and with such deep pathos. In his life we have an outstanding example of heat and light, both pathos and logos. It was ethos which would result in his tragic fall. Although supremely we are to look to David's greater Son, it is in observing the life of a fellow struggler with sin such as the 'sweet singer of Israel' that we can perhaps derive most encouragement. In order to speak with divine pathos, we need—as Bounds put it—a 'heart in tune with

God and in sympathy with the people'. We see this in David. Even in some of his darkest and most distressing moments, his noble heart and genuine concern for others is evident. Fleeing for his life from Jerusalem after his son Absalom's ruthless rebellion, he says magnanimously to Ittai the Gittite and the men with him, 'Go back and stay with King Absalom. You are a foreigner, an exile from your homeland. You came only yesterday. And today shall I make you wander about with us, when I do not know where I am going? Go back, and take your people with you. May the Lord show you kindness and faithfulness' (2 Sam. 15:19–20). It is perhaps significant that while there are fourteen chapters of the Bible concerned with the great patriarch Abraham, no fewer than sixty-two chapters are devoted to the life of David.

Child-like humility

Though we could mention a number of outstanding qualities of his which we might aspire to—such as his courage, faith and godly devotion—it is his deep, unfeigned humility and child-likeness we might benefit most from when considering the subject of pathos. For example, we read that 'King David went in, sat before the Lord, and said, "Who am I, O, Sovereign Lord, and what is my family, that you have brought me this far?"' (2 Sam. 7:18). Bear in mind this was just after being told he would not be the one to build the temple. He is not smarting or sulking, feeling slighted that God should by-pass him and favour another. Instead, he is overwhelmed by God's grace and goodness towards him. Spurgeon remarks, 'David's sense of his own nothingness is strikingly set forth'. We see this same child-like humility in the life of the great Apostle also. Paul saw himself as 'the least of the apostles' (1 Cor. 15:9) and even, 'less than the least of all the saints' (Eph. 3:8). There is something both powerful and attractive in such genuine self-effacing ministry. This is far from today's obsession with self. How am *I* performing? How am *I* perceived by others? How popular am *I?* It is ministry (so called) driven by that cancerous desire for approval, praise, and preferment, the very opposite of gospel humility that should adorn every preacher. 'Humility is not thinking less of yourself; it is thinking of yourself less', said one perceptively.[2] The phrase is often attributed, most probably incorrectly, to C.S. Lewis. The nearest Lewis gets to this is in *Mere Christianity* where he writes, 'It is better to forget about yourself altogether'.[3]

Pathos in preaching is that throb of human love and genuine concern for those to whom we are addressing, so that hearers sense this affection pulsating throughout the message. It is such an attitude that the Holy Spirit delights to own and supplement with divine pathos. We must pray that we will be so large-hearted that our words come clothed with this mysterious self-oblivious power, an unaffected pathos which disarms and breaks down any barriers of objection, opposition or indifference—and that even breaks down barriers of age, those times when children are among those listening. If there is any key in being able to hold the interest of children in preaching it perhaps is due to the warm, self-effacing, child-like character of the preacher. The greatest preachers, even those of significant intellect, seem to possess a magnetic ability in drawing and holding the interest of children. To some, Martyn Lloyd-Jones ('The Doctor!') appeared an austere, even intimidating figure but that perception was far from reality. Children not only enjoyed his ministry, but felt free to approach him. He once received a letter from a young girl in the congregation who wrote to him during a short absence to say that she hoped he would soon be back because he was 'the only preacher she could understand'.[4] It is this dual impact of word and life that creates a lasting impression. I happened to be preaching in a church in the south of England and was given hospitality for the day by a godly and gracious couple. Over lunch the wife, who was a former member of Westminster Chapel in London, spoke not only of Lloyd-Jones's powerful preaching but also of his accessibility and warmth of character. It transpired she (then in her sixties) was that 'young girl' who wrote to the preacher!

Men for the hour

Ours is the privilege of being able to draw on over 2000 years of preaching examples and mentors. Yet whilst seeking to emulate them, we dare not seek to replicate them. Let us be careful to avoid the trap of being clones

A heart after God's own

or echoes of any preacher—past or present. Great hearts make great preachers and let us by all means catch the flame of pathos that burned in their hearts. May we have the same desire and determination as Spurgeon when he said:

> I am occupied in my small way, as Mr Great-heart was employed in Bunyan's day. I do not compare myself with that champion, but I am in the same line of business. I am engaged in personally-conducted tours to Heaven... I am often afraid of losing some of the weaklings. I have the heart-ache for them; but, by God's grace, and your kind and generous help in looking after one another, I hope we shall all travel safely to the river's edge. Oh, how many have I had to part with there! I have stood on the brink, and I have heard them singing in the midst of the stream, and I have almost seen the shining ones lead them up the hill, and through the gates, into the Celestial City.[5]

No matter how far short we think we fall, how hard and shrunken we feel our hearts to be, the reality is, we are indwelt by Mr Great-Heart, our Lord Jesus himself. He asks only that we stay close to him so that we may receive from him and then communicate something of his heart to needy souls. E.M. Bounds again encourages us, that the need of the hour is not great preachers, '... but men great in holiness, great in faith, great in love, great in faithfulness, great for God—men always preaching by holy sermons in the pulpit, by holy lives out of it. These men can mould a generation for God.'[6]

APPENDIX 1: PATHOS ON THE STREETS

There are many who have deep concerns regarding the relevance and/or appropriateness of preaching in the open-air in our day, especially when it comes to what is often referred to as 'street evangelism'. As one who is convinced of the primacy of preaching outside as well as inside church buildings and fully persuaded of its effectiveness, I do understand, however, why such reservations exist. We all have seen poor, and sadly even verbally aggressive examples of street preaching. Being so public makes it appear doubly inexcusable. Sincere as they may be, the approach and manner of some preachers can be lacking the essential grace, winsomeness—and in the context of this book, the pathos that is so essential for such a delicate and difficult ministry. But should we so easily jettison such a time-honoured and potentially fruitful means of reaching total outsiders with the gospel? Are we satisfied as churches that we are doing all in our power to reach multitudes who are living and dying without Christ, therefore without hope? Whilst being only too aware of the necessity of bridge-building and befriending, the Apostle Paul challenges us, 'How shall they hear without someone preaching to them?' (Rom. 10:14). As one who has been engaged in open-air work for over forty years, I believe I have made enough mistakes to be of use to any who desire to make Christ known to an ever-increasingly spiritually ignorant and desperately needy generation through open-air preaching. The following comes with my heartfelt prayer that it may increase the effectiveness of those already engaged in this great work, as well as change the thinking of those who remain to be persuaded. Let us start by considering the benefits of this ministry and then move on to the method and manner.

Advantages of open-air street evangelism

Let us begin by considering its unique nature.

Open-air work:
- Reaches all types and classes of people
- Reaches all ages of people
- Reaches across nationalities and cultures
- Reaches those who would never go to church
- Reaches those who are not allowed to go to a church because of religious or cultural barriers
- Reaches those who have no Christian family, friends, colleagues or contacts
- Helps detect those in whom spiritual desires are stirring
- Makes known the requirements of God and the salvation of God
- Keeps believers in touch with how the 'man in the street' thinks (especially important for preachers)[1]
- Drives us to prayer and to study the Scriptures more urgently
- Is a means of unifying believers on the essentials for the gospel's sake

Appendix 1

- Is a great training ground for young preachers and gospel workers.
- Has a reviving effect upon our own souls[2]

Method and manner

1. Team work

Ideally, each church would have their own open-air team engaging on a regular basis in their locality—providing the location is appropriate for street outreach.[3] If not possible, then those who are engaged in a team should be committed to a local church or assembly, and gladly under the authority of its leaders (Heb. 13:17). 'Lone wolves' should be discouraged. Sadly, so often there are individuals who are, for whatever reason, not subject to a local church leadership. This work is not just about someone preaching, and is always most effective when there is a mixed team of believers working in humility and harmony. It is a great witness to an unbelieving world in itself when men and women of mixed age, colour and culture join together as one. We are on a rescue mission. Secondary doctrinal issues and differences are pushed to one side as we link arms and join together in a warfare which is more deadly, with consequences that far greater, than any mortal conflict. Team members must not be considered 'supporting actors' in the work! Personal work is vitally important. D.L. Moody said, 'The best sermons are where one person is the preacher and one person the congregation.' This is not to diminish the priority and function of the preaching of the word in any way. But it is in one-to-one conversations you get to hear just where a person is and can apply the gospel more accurately and intimately. 'The best fruit is hand-picked', commented Spurgeon, and the more people involved in the 'picking' the greater the chance of fruit.

2. Preacher's credibility

Spirit-filled preaching has the power to arrest and draw people. But the preacher's initial aim is to connect with his hearers. Our first task is to gain their attention, before even attempting to address their hearts and minds. This is challenging enough in a pulpit over a period of thirty to forty minutes, but it takes twice the effort to achieve in a street setting, where we are not known and have no credibility or point of reference whatsoever. We convey the gospel in words, but by much more than words. From the very start, we need an awareness that even before a word is heard, people will look at us and make judgments. We cannot afford to be self-conscious, but we do need to be self-aware and give thought to how we appear to the unsuspecting public who will likely view open-air preaching as a strange spectacle as they pass by. People must be able to take one look at us, even from a distance and think, 'I don't know what that guy's saying, but he seems a pretty sane, normal, reasonable person.' We aim to arouse curiosity, but in a positive way!

3. Hook

All preachers, whether inside or outside a church building, need a 'hook' when opening their message. That is, right from start of our message, hearers will say inwardly, 'I'm interested in this. There is something here for me.' But in open-air work, it is so much harder as we have no waiting audience—they have their minds set on anything and everything but listening to a 'religious sermon'! But you yourself are part of that hook and we have just seconds to convince people we have something to say of interest and relevance. And importantly, we need to look as though we ourselves have been affected by the good news! As Spurgeon said, 'There are many more flies caught with honey than with vinegar and there are many more sinners brought to Christ by happy Christians than by doleful Christians!'[4] And of course, many will not have been present for the start of our message, so there should be a repetitive, recapping, cyclical approach to our method, yet with freshness.

4. Dress

We don't want to be pernickety here, but how we dress does matter and thought must be given to it. Generally, our aim should be to blend into our particular setting rather than unhelpfully stand out. First impressions can either help or hinder the preacher and his message. Let us avoid the 'weirdometer' registering any more than it ought!

5. Speech and Language

To be sure, the dynamics of public preaching are different to a conversational one-to-one sharing of the gospel. Preaching is proclamation, but let us beware of creating an unnecessary gulf between us.

Preaching the Heart of God

Avoid a condemning, declaiming style

We pray that the Holy Spirit will give us boldness in our preaching and that our words will be clothed with his convicting and converting power. But we must avoid a strident, aggressive or judgmental style. Some street preachers say they are preaching in love, but can come over as quite hostile.[5]

Also, we can have the right message, but the wrong attitude. 'We are not Old Testament prophets', says Roger Carswell, 'we have been given a different message to proclaim, the good news of Jesus.'[6] We must make the gospel sound like the good news that it is.

Be aware

Pay close attention to those occasions when having to compete with surrounding noise (traffic or buskers, for example) as very often the louder we try to speak, the more our faces are likely to contort, giving off an angry look, even if we are not. The louder we speak, the harsher we may sound. There is a difference between shouting and projecting one's voice naturally.

Tips

- Beware of your 'off days'! (Disagreement with spouse, problems parking the car etc.)
- Be careful on those days when there is little response—apart from comments made that undermine your confidence and make you feel defensive and vulnerable!

Appendix 1 ➡

- Remember, in rejecting us, people are not necessarily rejecting Christ

Be natural and personal in your preaching

It is helpful for the preacher to think to himself, 'How would I speak if my unconverted cousin, mum or friend from work was passing by? What tone of voice would I use?'

Language

The words we use must be jargon-free ... and intelligible.

We know what we mean by terms like 'sin', 'salvation', 'eternal life', 'Heaven' and 'Hell', but what does that mean to a pagan Westerner? Simple Anglo-Saxon English, spoken clearly and at a good pace is helpful not only for British folk but is essential for non-native English speakers in our communities.

Tone of voice

Our tone must be attractive. No shouting or ranting! Spurgeon comments timelessly:

The best street preaching is not that which is done at the top of your voice, for it is impossible to lay the proper emphasis upon telling passages when all along you are shouting with all your might ... A quiet, penetrating, conversational style would seem to be most telling. Men do not bawl or halloa when they are pleading in deepest earnestness ... Less rant and a few more tears.[7]

Evangelist J.P. Earnest often says, 'I prefer to preach *to* people not *at* people.' There is a big difference between throwing a ball to someone and throwing a ball *at* them!

Be wise in choice of location and avoid:

- Too narrow a street—your voice may sound extra loud and intrusive.
- Too wide a space where there is nothing to use as a sounding board for your voice (and easier for people to give you a 'wide berth'!).
- Speaking as though addressing the whole city ('Good afternoon Birmingham!') But speak as if addressing just one person.
- Use of amplification if possible. The aim is to draw people to us not keep at a distance.
- Setting up near vendors, buskers or anyone whose income could be affected. Choose somewhere where you are not likely to cause obstruction or offence.

6. Eye contact

Speak personally and try to make a point of looking at people in their eyes; not staring, but warm, natural eye-contact. Think as you preach, 'She could be my gran. He could be my wayward brother. She could be my rebellious niece, that furrow-browed businessman could be about to take his life.' People should be able to detect we have a genuine concern for *them* and eye contact can help draw people in to listen further.

7. Visual aids

A display board that uses captions and Scripture can be a real help. The pace of life is frantic and we want to slow people down, catch their attention and cause them to think about eternal things. John Bunyan spoke of two main channels into the human mind, 'Ear Gate' and 'Eye Gate'.

Developing a talk or explaining a Bible verse with laminated captions:

- Displays a structured and reasoned argument for the gospel.
- Adding each caption as the message develops has the 'curiosity' factor and can help draw people and maintain their attention.
- Helps the preacher to keep to the point (like sermon notes in a pulpit).
- Continues to preach from the board even when the preacher has finished!

8. Hecklers

Good hecklers are worth their weight in gold, and can be a great means in helping to draw a crowd, but we need to handle them with great grace and wisdom. However, if the heckler is one who gives no opportunity for you to speak, then terminate the conversation (not the heckler!). Be sure to be gracious and polite at all times, your response will likely be being closely examined by others. Very often we fail to win the heckler but gain the sympathy and interest of those who stopped to see the 'action'. At all times, we must seek to win our hearers with a 'cocktail' of love and logic. Onlookers closely observe in a pressure situation not just what we say but how we say it in our response to a heckler.

> Preaching the Heart of God

9. Remember the source of power—the cross of our Lord Jesus Christ!

Let us learn from the Apostle Paul's great conviction: 'I resolved to know nothing while I was with you except Jesus Christ and him crucified' (1 Cor. 2:2). When we have done our best to present our arguments, and be as appealing as we can, we are praying for a miracle from heaven to convict of sin, open blind eyes, unstop deaf ears and convert hearts of stone to flesh. Only God can make dead people live and although the preaching of the cross is 'foolishness to those who are perishing' (1 Cor. 1:18), it is at the heart of God's saving work, and the Holy Spirit uniquely honours the preaching of Christ crucified. And risen! Never forget to preach the resurrection.

10. Know when to end the message

I've seen men with a good crowd, and thought at a certain point, 'This would be the time to close' (i.e. urge them to repent and trust Christ and offer a gospel or other literature). But the preacher goes on ... and on ... and on ... and the crowd drifts away. Opportunity lost.

Finally ... Go!

> We go in faith, our own great weakness feeling...
>
> –Edith G. Cherry

May I plead:

For the pastors and leaders of local churches, in their evangelistic considerations to think of the possibility of setting apart a group of their best Christians. Warm,

Spirit-filled men and women who overflow with love, grace, compassion and humility who would be willing to venture out into those pedestrian town centres where vast numbers of people pass by each day. Book tables can be laid out with a wide variety of attractive literature. Warm, winsome open-air preaching will go hand in hand with this beautifully. One-to-one conversations are often ignited through a simple leaflet offered with a friendly smile. Let us not be deterred by any poor examples we have seen (we no doubt have also experienced deficient preaching inside churches, yet still hold firmly to the primacy of preaching!). Yes, there is a cost involved in standing for Christ publicly, but also a Holy Spirit empowering joy. I am convinced that being involved in this sort of outreach work has a personal reviving effect. And what could be more thrilling than seeing large groups of warm-hearted gospel people on our streets, overflowing with pathos and showing by their humble boldness that there is real hope in this increasingly dark world and that Jesus really is alive and willing to save?

For preachers involved in this great work, to work pray and work continually regarding our manner as we go as men who have been forgiven much to those in need of being forgiven much. It was said of our Saviour, 'all spoke well of him and were amazed at the gracious words that came from his lips.' May we be filled with the Spirit and go out with that same grace.

For further help or information regarding open-air ministry visit: www.oamission.com

→ Preaching the Heart of God

APPENDIX 2: TEN ESSENTIAL BOOKS FOR YOUNG PREACHERS

Power through Prayer, E.M. Bounds
An essential read for one setting out in preaching as it drives home the vital, indissoluble relationship between prayer and true preaching and that preaching has no power without being backed up by a life of prayer. Bounds' book carries a fragrance of heaven which has the effect of percolating into the reader's mindset.

Preaching and Preachers, M. Lloyd-Jones
This perhaps is the first book to read on preaching as Lloyd-Jones sets out before us what preaching actually is and what the preacher should be aiming to do. The centrality and primacy of preaching is systematically presented in a passionate, inspiring, anecdotal and of course, biblical way.

Preaching Pure and Simple, S. Olyott
The best practical book on preaching. It does exactly what the title says and gives the young preacher setting out a pattern for life, as well as reminding more mature preachers of the essential components of good preaching. Full of spiritual wisdom.

Lectures to My Students, C.H. Spurgeon
Stimulating, provocative, humorous. Don't be put off by content that seems so culturally far from us, but drink

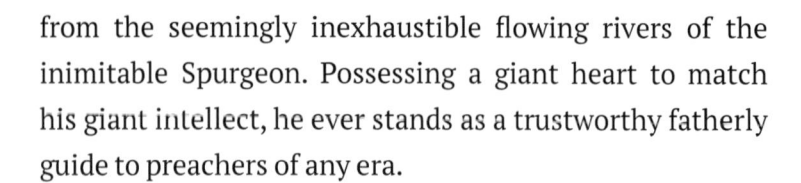

from the seemingly inexhaustible flowing rivers of the inimitable Spurgeon. Possessing a giant heart to match his giant intellect, he ever stands as a trustworthy fatherly guide to preachers of any era.

I Believe in Preaching, J. Stott
Stott very helpfully sets preaching in its wider context and begins with a historical outline which then moves into dealing with the issue of contemporary objections to God's primary mode of communicating his word. As well as dealing with preaching as bridge-building, he finally shows the importance of the man's character and his working pattern.

Evangelistic Preaching, R. Carswell
Every preacher and pastor is called to 'do the work of an evangelist' and Carswell reminds us that we should be on guard never to let this element in our ministry slip. His little book is a stimulating spur to ensure we never lose sight of those among our hearers who need to clearly hear on a regular basis how they may be saved.

Speaking in Public Effectively, R. Bewes
Bewes, in an enormously practical and stimulating way helps us to take a wider look at the whole matter of verbal communication. A great help for those of us who are 'of a nervous disposition' launching out in the work of public speaking and who need gently leading by the hand.

The Supremacy of God in Preaching, J. Piper
This is like a refresher for those who have benefited from reading 'Preaching and Preachers' and want to capture something of the greatness of God and of the awesome privilege of coming with 'gravity and gladness' (Piper) to make him known to others.

An All Round Ministry, C.H. Spurgeon
What is said about Lectures to my Students (above) is equally true of this gem also.

Seeing Beauty and Saying Beautifully, J. Piper
It is not just what the preacher says, but how he says it, and Piper seeks to awaken us from lazy ways of delivering words to convince us that because words are powerful, we will actually give thought and attention to them. He does this in a mouth-watering way by using poet George Herbert, evangelist George Whitefield and writer/academic C.S. Lewis to demonstrate the impact their speech had, and still has today.

There is no shortage of excellent books on preaching, and this is simply a 'starter' list of books I consider essential in shaping a young preacher's mindset – as well as being books the mature preacher will return to time and again.

Although in no particular order, you will notice at the top of the list is actually, a book on prayer. The apostolic priority was that they would give themselves 'continually to prayer and to the ministry of the word' (Acts 6:4). I know of no greater place for an aspiring preacher to start his journey than Power through Prayer by E.M. Bounds. It is one of these books we feel the need to return to time and again throughout our entire lives and ministry. It is full of life, warmth and incentive to pray.

ENDNOTES

INTRODUCTION

1. C.H. Spurgeon, 'Sermon on John 11:35', 23 June 1889 https://www.spurgeon.org/resource-library/sermons/jesus-wept/#flipbook/
2. Haddon Robinson, *Making a Difference in Preaching* (Grand Rapids: Baker Books, 1999), p. 82.
3. Mostyn Roberts, London Seminary website, 14 May 2019 https://londonseminary.org/blog/mostyn-roberts-on-the-three-hearts-of-preaching/
4. Quoted in an article by Kieran Beville, *The Banner of Truth Magazine*, August–September 2003.
5. J.W. Alexander, *Expository Thoughts on Preaching* (Edinburgh: The Banner of Truth, 1975), p. 9.
6. Mez McConnell, Twitter, 14 November 2019. Note: 20schemes' long term desire is to see Scotland's housing schemes transformed by the gospel of Jesus Christ through the planting of gospel-preaching churches, ultimately led by a future generation of indigenous church leaders.' For more information visit https://20schemes.com

CHAPTER 1

1. A.W. Tozer, *The Best of A.W. Tozer* (Grand Rapids: Baker Books, 1978), p. 141.
2. C.H. Spurgeon, *Lectures to My Students* (Grand Rapids: Baker Books, 1980), p. 13.
3. Warren W. Wiersbe, *The Wiersbe Bible Commentary* (Colorado Springs: David C. Cook, 2007), p. 777.
4. John Angell James, *An Earnest Ministry* (Edinburgh: The Banner of Truth, 1993), p. 57.

CHAPTER 2

1. John Stott, *I Believe in Preaching* (London: Hodder & Stoughton, 1982), p. 276.
2. Richard Bewes Speaking in Public Effectively (Inverness: Christian Focus, 2002), pp. 83, 85.
3. Jonathan Mason is a Lay reader in Holy Trinity Church, Norwich http://www.walkingwithgiants.net/preaching/modes-of-persuasion-ethos-pathos-logos/
4. Martyn Lloyd-Jones, *Preaching and Preachers* (London: Hodder & Stoughton, 2013), p. 87.
5. 'Rhetoric', *The American Heritage Dictionary of the English Language*, fourth edition (Boston: Houghton Mifflin, 2006).
6. Quoted by John Piper, *Seeing Beauty and Saying Beautifully* (Wheaton: Crossway, 2014), p. 31.
7. Macneile Dixon quoted in Warren Wiersbe, *Preaching with Imagination* (Grand Rapids: Baker Books, 1994), p. 87.
8. John Piper, *The Supremacy of God in Preaching* (Grand Rapids: Baker Books, 1990), pp. 49–50.

9 John Wesley, *The Journal of John Wesley* (Chicago: Moody Publishers, 1951), p. 169.

Chapter 3

1 J.I. Packer, 'What Do You Mean When You Say God?', *Christianity Today* (Sept 1986) 31:27–31 https://www.monergism.com/divine-impassibility-0

2 Packer, 'What Do You Mean When You Say God?', 31:27–31.

3 Dane Ortland, *Gentle and Lowly* (Wheaton: Crossway, 2020), p. 73.

4 Donald Macleod, 'Does God have feelings?' Personal Blog, 9 December 2019 https://donaldmacleod.org.uk/dm/does-god-have-feelings/

5 Calvin's Commentaries, *Isaiah*, https://biblehub.com/commentaries/calvin/isaiah/63.htm

Chapter 4

1 Spoken of Bishop Hugh Latimer and quoted in, Stott *I Believe in Preaching*, p. 26.

2 Roger Carswell, *Evangelistic Preaching* (Leyland: 10Publishing, 2020), p. 26.

3 Jerry Vines and Adam B. Dooley, *Passion in the Pulpit* (Chicago: Moody Publishers, 2018), p. 27.

4 Quoted by Steven Lawson in a blog, 'George Whiefield's love for Christ and Sinners' https://www.ligonier.org/blog/george-whitefields-love-christ-and-sinners/

5 Ortland, *Gentle and Lowly*, p. 13.

6 Stott, *I Believe in Preaching*, p. 265.

7 Vines and Dooley, *Passion in the Pulpit*, p. 56.

Chapter 5

1 Quoted in *Preaching is More than Telling the Truth* available at https://www.sermoncentral.com/pastors-preaching-articles/peter-mead-preaching-is-more-than-telling-the-truth-1417

2 Martyn Lloyd-Jones, *The Puritans* (Edinburgh: The Banner of Truth, 1987), p. 360.

3 C.H. Spurgeon, *The Soul Winner*, Kindle Edition, Location 158.

4 Stuart Olyott, *Preaching Pure and Simple* (Bridgend: Bryntirion Press, 2005), p. 151.

5 John Newton, *Letters of John Newton* (Edinburgh: The Banner of Truth 1976), p. 51.

6 Olyott *Preaching Pure and Simple*, pp. 122–3.

7 F.W. Boreham, *A Late Lark Singing* available at https://www.fwboreham.com/books-by-fwb/1945-a-late-lark-singing/the-secret-of-murray-mccheyne/

8 Geoffrey Thomas available at http://geoffthomas.org/index.php/gtsermons/preaching-2-the-man/

9 Roger Carswell, 'Henry Moorhouse', *Evangelical Times*, August 2018 https://www.evangelical-times.org/43935/henry-moorhouse/

Endnotes

Chapter 6

1. Andrew A. Bonar, *Memoir and Remains of R.M. M'Cheyne* (Edinburgh: The Banner of Truth, 1978), p. 43.
2. Quoted by Sinclair Ferguson at https://www.desiringgod.org/articles/preach-like-hell-lasts-forever
3. Maurice Roberts, 'Christ Weeping Over Jerusalem', *The Banner of Truth Magazine*, August 2003 https://banneroftruth.org/uk/resources/articles/2003/christ-weeping-over-jerusalem/
4. Cited by David Mathis in a Desiring God article 'O, the deep, deep joy of Jesus' https://www.desiringgod.org/articles/oh-the-deep-deep-joy-of-jesus
5. C.H. Spurgeon, 'Sermon on Psalm 45:7—The Oil of Gladness', 16 January 1876 https://www.ccel.org/ccel/spurgeon/sermons22.iii.html
6. Stuart Olyott, *Ministering Like the Master* (Edinburgh: The Banner of Truth, 2003), p. 67.
7. Ortland, *Gentle and Lowly*, p. 99.
8. Quoted by Roger Carswell, *Evangelistic Living*,
9. Robert Sheehan, 'God's Love to the Non-Elect', *Reformation Today*, May/June 1995.
10. Iain H. Murray, *Heroes* (Edinburgh: The Banner of Truth, 2009), pp. 272, 274.
11. Iain H. Murray, *Wesley and Men who Followed* (Edinburgh: The Banner of Truth, 2003), pp. 149, 150, 175.
12. Amy Carmichael, 'Towards Jerusalem' (London: SPCK, 1987), p. 85.

Chapter 7

1. Stuart Olyott speaking about Hywel Griffiths in *Something Must be Known and Felt* (Bridgend: Evangelical Movement of Wales, 2014), p. 9.
2. Quoted in an article by Kieran Beville, *The Banner of Truth Magazine*, August–September, 2003.
3. Lloyd-Jones, *Preaching and Preachers*, p. 324.
4. E.M. Bounds, *Power Through Prayer* (New Jersey: Barbour and Company, 1984), pp. 67–8.
5. Olyott, *Something Must be Known and Felt*, p. 9.
6. E.M. Bounds, *Power Through Prayer*, p. 9.
7. Michael Reeves, 'Did you know Charles Spurgeon Suffered from Depression?' https://www.crossway.org/articles/did-you-know-that-charles-spurgeon-struggled-with-depression/
8. Zack Eswine, *Kindled Fire* (Inverness: Christian Focus Publications, 2006), p. 99.
9. Bounds, *Power Through Prayer*, p. 10.

Chapter 8

1. Martyn Lloyd-Jones, *Logic on Fire*, DVD (Media Gratia, 2020).

2   Alistair Begg and Sinclair B. Ferguson, *Name Above All Names* (Wheaton: Crossway, 2013), p. 48.
3   Bruce Bickel, *Light and Heat—The Puritan View of the Pulpit* (Grand Rapids: Reformation Heritage Books, 1999), p. 30.
4   Stott, *I Believe in Preaching*, p. 273.
5   John MacArthur Foreword in Michael Fabarez, *Preaching that Changes Lives* (Nashville: Thomas Nelson, 2002).
6   Jeffrey Arthurs, *Place of Pathos in Preaching* https://www.preachingtoday.com/books/art-and-craft-of-biblical-preaching/delivery/place-of-pathos-in-preaching.html
7   Fanny Crosby, 'Rescue the Perishing', 1869.
8   E.M. Bounds, *Power Through Prayer*, p. 70.
9   David McIntyre quoting Dr. Moody Stuart, *The Hidden Life of Prayer* (Inverness: Christian Focus Publications, 2010), p. 18.
10 E.M. Bounds, *Power Through Prayer*, p. 23.
11 F.W. Faber, 'My God, how wonderful Thou art' (1814–1863).
12 Quoted in Wiersbe, *New Testament Commentary*, p. 788.

Epilogue

1   E.M. Bounds, *Power Through Prayer,* p. 10.
2   Quoted in Timothy Keller, *The Freedom of Self-forgetfulness* (Leyland: 10Publishing, 2012), p. 32.
3   C.S. Lewis, *Mere Christianity* (London: Collins, 2012), p. 125.
4   Iain H. Murray, *D. M. Lloyd-Jones: The Fight of Faith* (Edinburgh: The Banner of Truth, 1990), p. 630.
5   C.H. Spurgeon, 'Sermon Parable of the Innkeeper', available at https://www.metropolitantabernacle.org/Christian-Article/Parable-of-the-Inkeeper-Taking-Care-of-Others/Sword-and-Trowel-Magazine
6   E.M. Bounds *Power Through Prayer*, p. 11.

Appendix

1   All too often preachers are accused of being 'out of touch' with the real world and that it is evident in our preaching vocabulary, illustrations, presuppositions etc. Prof. Andy MacIntosh calls open-air work 'a spiritual thermometer testing where the nation is at' (https://youtu.be/BVaeQjmsp9k).
2   Engaging in open-air work is like jumping into a cool swimming pool on a sweltering hot day. It takes courage and commitment to jump in, but once in it is so refreshing!
3   In practice this means a larger town or city centre where there is sufficient space to avoid obstruction or any sense of intrusion and also where there is a decent flow of people.

Endnotes

4 C.H. Spurgeon. 'Sermon 2405—Joy, a Duty', 24 March 1895.

5 Spurgeon, in seeking to strongly emphasise the importance of sensitivity in our evangelistic preaching said, 'Many an earnest fool has driven a soul to hell in his endeavour to drag it to heaven by force; for human wills yield not to such rough force, but rebel the more. Souls have to be brought to salvation by a gentleness and wisdom such as the Saviour used when he fascinated the Samaritan woman into eternal life, and enticed her to the truth'. Sermon by C.H. Spurgeon, The Samaritan Woman and Her Mission, 10 September 1882 https://www.spurgeon.org/resource-library/sermons/the-samaritan-woman-and-her-mission/#flipbook/

6 Carswell, *Evangelistic Living*, p. 33.

7 Spurgeon, *Lecture to my Students*, p. 92.